THE HIDDEN ROADS

The Hidden Roads

A Memoir of Childhood

KEVIN CROSSLEY-HOLLAND

First published in Great Britain in 2009 by Quercus

21 Bloomsbury Square
London
WC1A 2NS

A CIP catalogue reference for this book is available
from the British Library

ISBN 978 1 84724 736 0

10 9 8 7 6 5 4 3 2 1

Designed and typeset by Rook Books, London
Printed and bound in Great Britain by Clays Ltd, St Ives plc

Contents

Isn't He Awful!	1
My Mother and Father	4
Crosskeys	9
Whiteleaf Cross	14
Birthday Parties	20
In the Beechwoods	23
Biting Mrs Robertson	28
From Everlasting to Everlasting	31
The Invisible Worm	36
Grandpa Frank and Neenie	43
Switzerland	46
Sixty-Seven Small Faces	53
The 1948 Olympics	59
The Then and Now of It	61
Better Than All Books	69
Bicycling	75
Burnham Overy Staithe	81
In the Back Seat	90
Opera Fever	94
Singing Lessons	98
My Museum	102
'Where beth they, beforen us weren?'	108
Making Magic	111
Phew!	114
Swept up in the Dance	124
In Norfolk: Cometh the Hour . . .	131

Uncle Dick and Aunt Rosemary   138
Expecting the Best   142
The King is Dead. Long Live the Queen!   146
King Arthur   150
Massacre   151
French Exchanges   156
Black Waxworks   160
The Great Flood of 1953   164
Coaching at Lord's   170
Scout Camp   173
Beating and Initiation   179
Ice and Flame   184
Lifting my Eyes   187
Common Entrance   193
Happy Families   196
Every Man Needs a Tool   199
In Norfolk: Time, Tide and Tennis   201
On a Shoestring   209

Thresholds: Before and After   215

Acknowledgements   228

for my sister Sally

with love

Hrisebyrgan be cilternes efese: the brush-covered hills by the Chiltern eaves.

East Risborough Charter, AD 903

No concerts or lantern lectures, not even the fairy stories of Hans Andersen and the Brothers Grimm, were as entertaining and interesting to my sister and me as when our mother was a little girl . . . She was *awful*. But our confidence in her goodness never wavered.

Winifred Beechey, *The Rich Mrs Robinson*

Life without memory is no life at all . . . Our memory is our coherence, our reason, our feeling, even our action. Without it, we are nothing.

Luis Buñuel, *Memoirs*

And that's how we measure out our real respect for people – by the degree of feeling they can register, the voltage of life they can carry and tolerate – and enjoy . . . As Buddha says: live like a mighty river. And as the old Greeks said: live as though all your ancestors were living again through you.

Ted Hughes, writing to his son Nicholas, *Letters of Ted Hughes*

Isn't He Awful!

My first memory is of fury. I am two and alone in a room with a bawling baby in a pram. He is red-haired. In fact, everything about him is red – his face, his neck, his fingers, his toes. The longer he bawls, the redder he gets, and the redder he gets, the more angry I become.

I begin to shake the container of baby powder over him. A nursery snowfall. I shake it and shake it . . .

My second memory dates from much the same time, and it too is of fury.

I am with John, who is one year older than I am, and what he's saying (whatever it was!) is making me more and more angry. I pick up his favourite toy, his 'Noser Ark', and throw it at him. I miss. The wooden ark stoves in. The animals slip and slide all over the varnished, honey-coloured floor.

The third of my very early memories is of trying to keep up with my mother as she long-legs it down a steep street, urging me to hurry 'or else we'll miss the bus'. I keep complaining that there's something in my shoe, my foot's hurting, I can't go faster.

My mother told me that this happened when I was just

three. What is in the toe of my right shoe is a toothpaste cap.

My fourth memory is the most detailed. It took place in London later in the same year, during a German air raid.

I am a page at the wedding of my godmother, and I'm wearing gold satin trousers.

Before the reception at a London hotel, my parents and I go up to our room, and they leave me alone in the bathroom 'to cool down a bit'.

On the shelf above the wash-basin, there is a packet of Gillette razor-blades, each wrapped in oil paper. To while away the time, I undo them one by one. My mother finds me standing in the bath, surrounded by naked blades.

At the reception, I remember trotting around, offering guests pieces of wedding cake, and then sitting spellbound in front of the accordionist.

Somewhere outside, there is a loud bang (a V-1 or doodle-bug). The accordionist stops playing, the wedding party freezes. It was as if we were at a children's birthday party, playing statues, in which the first person to move is the loser. How long did everyone hold their breath? No more than two or three seconds, I suppose; but in my memory for ever. Now the accordion breathes again; it sings in the afterblast and the festivities resume, no doubt tempered and chastened.

I was born on Friday, 7 February 1941 in Richmond Lodge, a nursing home in Mursley in north Buckinghamshire. My mother was two weeks overdue and I arrived, she told me, at 10.55 a.m., 'just in time for a late breakfast'. I weighed 7 lb 14 1/2 oz.

The nurses at Mursley called me 'the professor'.

'Why?' I asked my mother.

'Because you looked so worried.'

My parents, however, called me Kevin (because my father was enamoured of the saint and the sound of that name) and then John (after the man who was supposedly my earliest known ancestor) and William (after my paternal grandfather, Frank William).

My mother's father, however, suggested tongue-in-cheek my second name should be Benghazi, the Libyan town that exchanged hands several times during the Second World War and was wrested back from the Germans on the day I was born.

Safely home, I was parked in my pram in the little sloping garden under the greengage tree.

One of my mother's friends peered into the pram, and very quickly pulled her head out again.

'Oh!' she said, shocked. 'Isn't he awful!'

Awful or not, I think I was healthy throughout my early childhood, but I had to wear shoes with built-up insteps. This is what Mr E. Flatow, M.Ch. Orth, FRCS, had to say:

TO WHOM IT MAY CONCERN

> KEVIN CROSSLEY-HOLLAND is suffering from knock knees and bilateral *pes valgus*. He requires stretchings of the knees, massage to the legs and foot exercises.

This splendidly terse, faintly absurd report anticipated later troubles.

My Mother and Father

My mother, Joan Mary, was born on 3 April 1912, in Peatling Magna in Leicestershire, and she was an only (and lonely) child. According to her 'Progress Book', her eyes were 'chameleonic mostly hazel' and her hair was silky, light brown and curly. She first stood 'quite alone' on 17 May 1913, 'never ailed a day' during the cutting of her teeth, and early inherited the peculiarity of 'saying "hm" like all Cowpers when addressed'! The first poem she learned to recite was 'Pussy cat, pussy cat, where have you been?'

My mother's dynamism, organisational skills and well-developed business sense she shared with her mother, Mary Bourne Collard; from her father, Claude Cowper, a general practitioner in Leighton Buzzard, she inherited quick wit – my father nicknamed her 'Funny' – and a sense of fair play.

Through her father, she was one-quarter Irish, but while she relished her descent from the Keoghs and Swinneys and Vere de Veres, she was firstly and proudly a child of middle-class Middle England and generations of farming stock. She delighted in the fact that one of her Collard forebears had ridden third in the formidable and dangerous Aylesbury Steeplechase (first run in 1836), that included a 'rattling good jump of 18 feet of naked water'.

My mother had a Roman nose, and her expressive eyes had a way of suddenly darkening. She often happily speculated whether Jewish blood had also entered the family's veins.

Although her own mother was a keen watercolourist, my mother's artistic achievement was of a different order. At the Central School of Art she studied under Dora Billington and, when she was twenty-five, began a highly promising career as a designer at Doultons art pottery in Lambeth. Her lovely, salt-glazed earthenware and stoneware, simple and generous and strong, won significant praise, and she was on four occasions a bronze or silver medallist of the Turner's Company. In January 1938, she showed off her skills on television, and the north Bedfordshire newspaper noted that she was 'the first local lady to appear in a television programme', and that 'many people gathered to watch the demonstrations in Messrs Griffin Bros. Showrooms, and were astonished to find the pictures and the voice so real'.

Writing a poem about the pottery made by Anasazi women, precursors of the Navajo and of twentieth-century potters such as Mary Martinez, I also had in my mind my mother's work:

> pots proud-breasted and wide-hipped,
> pot-bellied pots like melons and gourds,
> ample, kind and porous.
> Cream slip,
> black slip,
> orange on sepia,
> mouth-wide, womb-wide
> round as this poor planet
> we make, and break . . . *

My father, Peter, was four years younger than my mother. When, at the age of twenty-three, he graduated from the Royal

* *Selected Poems*: from 'Anasazi Women'.

5

College of Music where he had studied under John Ireland – 'J. I.', my father always called him – and won the Folie Prize for composition, it was also a prize for persistence. When my father had wanted to read Music at St John's College, Oxford, his father Frank refused to support him on both social and economic grounds. 'I have plans for my two sons,' he used to announce to his friends. 'I want them to qualify in two professions each – medicine and law.' So my father dutifully but resentfully read Medicine first instead.

My father was handsome in a Rupert Brooke kind of way; he had bright and merry blue eyes; he was a dreamer, as often as not listening to conversation with his eyes closed; he was gentle; he was philosophical, and later followed Ouspensky before turning to Vedanta and a guru in India; he was a contextualiser, a reconciler, who would go the long way round to avoid a scrap; he was a woman's man.

My parents' wedding in All Saints', Leighton Buzzard, on 30 September 1939, was reported in the local paper as being 'the biggest social event in the district for many months – certainly since the war began'. My mother 'looked really lovely in a gown of flowing cream satin, with cream Brussels lace veil framing her face, and a bouquet of arum lilies. At the heart-shaped neckline of the gown glimmered a diamond pendant, the gift of her mother.' The same paper faithfully described the outfits of many guests ('a black silk two-piece, the hip-length coat bordered with silver fox, and matching black cavalier hat . . . black edge-to-edge coat over powder-blue flannel, with black veiled hat . . . black, with a floral frock and multi-coloured spotted veil on her black hat . . .'). It also recorded that my spirited, forceful mother 'created a precedent' by electing to speak at her own wedding.

As a sort of dowry, Claude Cowper generously gave the newlyweds the hillside cottage of Crosskeys in the village of Whiteleaf, just above the spring line in the Chilterns. My father set about enlisting in one of the armed services and, with characteristic wholeheartedness, my mother relinquished her life as a potter. Eight months later, she was pregnant.

In actuality, my father tried to enlist in all three services, but was ruled out in each case because of a gastric ulcer. This complaint became seriously troublesome during and after the war years, but I was still aware that my father had been as much relieved as disappointed at his reprieve, and vaguely ashamed that he had not 'done his bit'.

When I was ten, one of my friends hit me in the solar plexus.

As we both emerged simultaneously from the stalls, Simon sighed and said with a beatific smile, 'Ahh! The second best thing in the world.'

I wasn't usually at a loss for words, but I didn't know how to reply to this one. I'd never heard anyone describe defecation before, let alone in such glowing terms; and if this was indeed the second best, what was the first?

'While I was sitting there,' Simon went on, 'I was wondering: what did your father do in the war?'

This was the question I had long dreaded and prepared for.

I put my left forefinger to my lips. 'Hush-hush!' I said.

In front of the speckled mirror, Simon carefully organised his kiss-curl. 'Wow!' he said.

What surprises me is that my tissue-thin answers to questions such as Simon's were never rumbled; what doesn't surprise me is that my father never once tried to protect me, to arm me by giving me chapter and verse; and what I still feel is slightly resentful and rather suspicious.

Sometime in 1942, my father took up a post with the Ministry of Food first in Oxford and then in Colwyn Bay, and in 1943 he was appointed north-west regional director (in Manchester) of CEMA, the Council for the Encouragement of Music and the Arts, forerunner of today's Arts Council.

So he and my mother reluctantly left Whiteleaf for a while, and moved first to North Wales, then to Whaley Bridge, and then to Wilmslow. At this last stop, my sister Sally joined the show. She was born in the Grosvenor Nursing Home in Heaton Moor, Stockport, on 24 January 1944, with eyes as blue as my father's, and was actually christened Zara (after my father's Romany great-grandmother, Zara or Sarah Tansey), Irene (after my father's mother), Mary (after my mother's mother).

'Sally on weekdays, Zara on Sundays,' my mother said. But that intention was largely observed in the breach.

Crosskeys

The theatre in which I played out my daily dreams, terrors, intense excitements, imaginings was in and around Crosskeys. Standing at the top of Westfield Road, it was penny-plain, steeply-roofed, built in the thirties, with half an acre of garden and a half-acre field at the bottom of which my father had dug two large vegetable plots. Hard work this was. As Clare Leighton wrote in *Four Hedges*, 'Its soil is chalk; its flower beds are pale grey. Dig into it just one spit, and you reach, as it were, a solid cement foundation.' Immediately behind the cottage rose Whiteleaf Hill and, cut out of its turf, the shining chalk cross, flanked by dense, ancient, luminous beechwoods.

When we returned to Crosskeys after the war ended, my sister Sally and I slept on bunk beds in the ground-floor nursery. I was on top, and played the pocket-general.

There, Sally and I lay and listened to my father retelling traditional tales, sometimes accompanying himself on his Welsh harp. An Anglo-Saxon half-line, *singan ond secgan* (to sing and say), suggests a way of reciting that is pitched but not melodic, and that's how my father told us stories: he sang-and-said them.

My father introduced us above all to Celtic fairy-tales: stories in which humans often have to observe rules and conditions set by fairyfolk and, when they fail to do so, pay the price of disrespect.

One of our favourites was the tale of Joan, the West Country farm-woman enlisted as a midwife! A small dark man rides her up to a hill-farm where his wife has just given birth, and when Joan disobeys his instructions and smears a little ointment intended for the baby on to her own right eyelid, she immediately sees that the woman and her dark husband are fairyfolk. Later, Joan spots the fairy man in the local market, stealing fruit:

'You can see me then?' said the little man.

Joan nodded.

'Which eye, Joan?' asked the little man, smiling.

Joan covered her left eye. She covered her right eye.

'This one,' she said.

The little dark man raised a hand and lightning flashed in Joan's right eye, a searing dazzle and then shooting stars and then complete darkness.

'That's for meddling!' cried the little man. 'That's for taking the ointment, Joan! You won't be seeing me again.'*

I read this tale now as a metaphor. We all live in the material world, and yet we all relish the yeast of imagination. We need both eyes. As a boy, I never doubted for one moment that there were lives and forces and presences around me: fairyfolk and wodwos in the beechwoods; the black dog Shuck, large as a donkey, roaming along the Norfolk saltmarshes where my grandparents lived; ghosts in the churchyard . . . That I would seldom or perhaps never see them made them no less real.

When we grew drowsy and my father slipped out – I never heard him step with a heavy tread in all his life – the burnt-orange tigers on the green canvas draw-down blind came to life. The blind itself trembled in the draught that flowed in

* *The Magic Lands: Folktales of Britain and Ireland*: from 'Fairy Ointment'.

around the window-frames, and the branches of the over-grown elder-bush tap-tapped at the window.

While I lay between waking and sleeping, my father sometimes sat down at his piano. I used to think the wide, strong, rising chords he began with (as a way of flexing his fingers and as an alternative to scales, maybe) were like stanchions or the feet of a great bridge straddling dangerous, dark water:

> at nights I heard
> you play – while you charmed babeldom I slept*

While my father was an imaginative storyteller, my mother was a witty raconteur, and she often used to fascinate, amuse and slightly scare me with Scenes from a Provincial Doctor's Life. Adjoining his surgery, she told us, her father had a whole room packed out with his medical instruments. She described them one by one, and in my febrile mind they became medieval torture weapons. Her father, she said, used to pick woodworm out of the oak beams with one of his hypodermic needles.

How often since then, when having my blood tested or being inoculated, have I wondered whether the needle might be blunt.

I was three when I watched my father carve a Christmas turkey, a great luxury in wartime, and I had no doubt that the carving-knife had come straight from the surgery.

'I don't like this fish,' I complained as soon as I'd tasted a mouthful.

At the top of our cottage's short, steep staircase there were two rooms, each with slatted, white wooden doors and black latches and locks.

My parents slept in the room on the left, and to begin with they shared a double bed. When I was nine, I graduated from the nursery to the room on the right.

My bedcover was a crimson blanket, and I still have it. It's ragged and full of holes, but I still can't bring myself to throw it away.

* *Selected Poems*: from 'Sounds'.

'A war-blanket,' my mother told me. 'Surplus stock. They dyed them this colour so you couldn't see the bloodstains.'

A little door in my upstairs bedroom led into the L-shaped space under the rafters we called the attic. Sally and I could just about stand up in it; my mother and father had to proceed on all fours.

The attic smelt of all the cooking-apples my mother laid out there; it was where overwintering hyacinth patiently bided their time. It was packed with memorabilia and the kind of junk that, because of its associations, is very difficult to chuck out.

Sally and I spent a great deal of time in there. It was our indoor hideaway, and a crossing-place between now and before. Just inside the door was an open cardboard box containing our hideous gas-masks. Years passed; the masks remained . . .

My mother told me about the Korean War (fought between 1950 and 1953 and still not officially over), and in particular about the killing of so many of the Gloucester Regiment.

Her gravity and sense of loss must have impressed themselves deeply on me and, lying under my crimson blanket, I had a recurring dream. The essentials were that I was walking out into desolate wilderness between the two facing armies, and calling out to them. In the name of children, children everywhere, I called on them, I begged them to make peace.

Such terrors, such imaginings . . . such memories. 'Our memory is our coherence,' Luis Buñuel wrote, 'our reason, our feeling, even our action.'

One night when I was seven, I was basking in the bath and my mother was sitting on the laundry-box beside me. We must have been talking about remembering and forgetting, and my mother asked me, quite urgently, 'Do you want to remember this place and this moment?'

'What do you mean?'

'For ever?'

'How?'

'By wanting to.'

I squirmed round to look at her over my right shoulder.

'By deciding to. By wanting to so much that there's nothing in your head and heart except this room, the window steamed-up, remember, this stool, look, your yellow towel, the square soap, you, me, these words . . .'

In her clearing of the mind and her focus, I suppose my mother was advocating something close to mindfulness. Elective memory! Over the years, I have often made use of it.

Whiteleaf Cross

Cut out of a hill all but eight hundred feet high, the bright beacon of Whiteleaf Cross is almost two hundred feet tall and as many feet across, and you can see it from very many miles away. In all likelihood, it was a prehistoric carving, possibly a phallus, 'converted' by medieval Benedictine monks. Christians have always been adept at baptising what they could not suppress.

On top of the hill was an oval Neolithic barrow, now dated to the thirty-seventh century BC, surrounded by wild raspberry bushes. And no more than two hundred yards in front of Crosskeys ran the astounding Neolithic track developed between BC 3000 and BC 1800 that begins its life as the Ridgeway in Wiltshire and Oxfordshire, vaults the Thames, and continues as the Upper and Lower Icknield Way through the Chilterns and up through Cambridgeshire into Norfolk:

Overseer of Epona and the fleet horses at Lambourn
the bigwigs in their hill-stations at Silbury and Chequers

Keeper of Dragon Hill and the craters on the bombing range
also the quaking grass the brome grass melilot and eyebright

Warden of the Og and the watercress beds and Goring Gap
the sarsens like dowdy sheep and dowdy sheep like sarsens

Custodian of the downs and brakes the strip lynchets and
   warrens
under the lapwing the glider's wing spring of yellow-hammers.*

Up and down and up and down! Sally and I knew each square foot of the Cross, especially its philtrum, and we regarded it as our own.

Once, we returned from holiday to find it crawling with boy scouts whose summer task it was to weed it and edge it. I was incensed; they were trespassers.

'Look at it, though!' my mother exclaimed. 'Gleaming!'

In my heart and mind, Whiteleaf Cross had always gleamed; and as the years pass, wherever I am, it still does.

In the beech-glade just over the top of the hill stood my climbing-tree. It was gnarled and knotted; and once I hid high up in it, terrified, while the village boys held a council of war below me. What will happen if they look up and see me? What will they do to me?

For years I've had a recurring nightmare of hiding in an oak chest in a room guarded by one Nazi. He is sitting on the far side of the room with a rifle between his knees. If I can be vigilant and the Nazi eventually falls asleep . . . but if I so much as move, let alone cough or sneeze . . .

And again: I run through the trees, and it's not a comforting beechwood; it is a dark, spiky pine forest.

She is behind me, the witch. I can hear her panting growing louder and louder.

Just when I think there's no hope, and she'll catch me, I see a round tower, pencil-thin, very high. Salvation! I rush in through the door, and begin to climb the circular steps. Up, up!

But the witch follows me in. As I climb, it dawns on me that my salvation is my prison, closing round my ears. There is no way

* *The Painting-Room*: from 'Above the Spring Line'.

15

back – only round and round and on and up. And at the top . . .

Up! Up these saucer steps!

I can hear her shallow breathing.

This is when I wake up.

This Hansel-and-Gretel-and-Rapunzel nightmare! This night-hag: she has regularly reappeared and chased and frightened me throughout my life.

Up in my climbing-tree, I felt the same freezing terror.

But there, I carved my initials. There, we whiled away the time with friends. And there, Sally and I sat and bounced on the stooping branch so supple that one moment our feet swept the ground, the next we were six feet off it.

The beechwoods were full of secret places, and after Bruce, our bull-terrier, had joined the family when I was six and Sally three, we were allowed to roam for hours at a time in a manner almost unthinkable now:

> This is the path I'll take today.

> This is the stile
> where once and only once
> I found white violets
> that straddles the path I'll take today.

> And this is the stump of a pollarded willow:
> it gave six poles to build the stile
> where once and only once
> I found white violets
> that straddles the path I'll take today.*

Standing on that stile, clutching white violets, Sally and I used to yell across the spacious valley to Bledlow Ridge (properly Bledlow Cop but we called it Ridge), all of three miles away. Mysteriously, our voices came back to us, distorted and disembodied.

Sometimes, Sally or I returned home without the other; and

* *The Painting-Room*: 'Every Stile and Stump'.

when this happened, Bruce had been trained to go and search for us.

'Go and find Kevin!' my parents instructed him. Or else: 'See Sally!'

Away Bruce galloped, barking and searching, never coming back without one or other of us in tow. It seemed unremarkable then. As young children, we take such wonders as everyday, and turn the everyday into wonders.

A few years ago, I was talking to the top year in a primary school. I put an apple on the table in front of them.

'Don't tell me it's green and round,' I said. 'I can see that. What else can you tell me about this apple?'

Silence. And then one girl cautiously volunteered, 'It'll cry if you bite it.'

Another said: 'It's freckled.'

And another: 'And speckled.'

And a fourth: 'It's like a sphere.'

'What else?' I asked.

Silence. And then a fifth girl ventured, 'Well, it's got these pips inside it.'

'What are they like?' I asked.

'Dark.'

'They're hidden, aren't they?'

'I've got it!' the girl said excitedly. 'They're like secrets.'

Isn't this eye, not looking but seeing, and isn't this ear, not listening but hearing, what underlies the Native American belief that each stick and stone in our universe has its own voice? And isn't it precisely this seeing eye, this focus, that lies at the heart of my mother's bathroom-words about desire, specificity and memory?

Wherever Sally and I roamed, we tended to gravitate – or, rather, levitate – to the hilltop before returning home.

When I was nine and becoming increasingly interested in archaeology, I began to kick over the new molehills there (as I still do, wherever I am), hoping to find a potsherd or, better, a coin.

And then Sally and I would stretch out on the springy, cropped turf or else sit side by side, Bruce panting beside us, our legs dangling over the top of the Cross.

In front of us lay the most magnificent, vast dreamscape, called by the painter John Nash 'the finest view in the south of England'. Field by field and hedge by hedge, house by house, almost tree by tree, Sally and I used to piece it and plot it – south-west towards Bledlow and the smoking cement-works at Chinnor; west, beyond Thame towards Oxford; north across to Aylesbury.

Here on the hilltop is where I first began to understand that, in the novelist Peter Vansittart's words, 'England is an old house packed with memories'. And trying to imagine what it would have been like to have lived here generations or even centuries ago, I closed my eyes and opened my eyes and began to remove elements I knew not to be ancient: council estates, the cement-works, the railway lines with their toy steam engines and brown-and-green carriages, flashing greenhouses . . .

Often and again, as not only the distance but the whole world started to turn blue, my reverie was interrupted by the insistent ringing of a bronze Alpine cowbell I still keep in the bedroom in case of emergency. Hundreds of feet below, my mother had come out of the cottage into our little garden and, standing beside our Alpine rockery, she was summoning us home.

Now and then we rebelled against my mother and father because of their endless rules, many of which we thought unnecessary or unfair. When I was seven and Sally four, I decided I'd had enough. I persuaded my sister it was time to leave home.

How easily children take actions all the more drastic because they do not anticipate consequence. Sally and I both packed small, shiny brown leather suitcases and hid them under our beds. At dusk, we slipped out of the cottage and hid in the lower field.

There, we sat on our suitcases because the grass was already dew-damp. We ignored my mother's calls and her clanging cow-bell.

As soon as it was decently dark, we scuttled a few yards down the lane to our next-door neighbour, Miss Lloyd, trusting that she would understand and take us in for the night, and help us to make a getaway early next morning.

My mother's response was robust and practical. As soon as we had got dressed the next morning: 'Now why don't you go and pick some wild strawberries to put on your porridge?' And my father was entirely calm. He too talked of something else, as if nothing untoward had happened. Then he retreated into his study, and played pacific, arching chords on his baby grand piano. Only later, I suppose, did our parents discuss with us what we had done, and I have no memory of it, but this small rebellion must have put them on their mettle and shocked them.

Birthday Parties

I have been thinking about Edmund Waller, a gentle, fair-haired boy with whom I went to school up to the age of nine. He and I were friends, and I remember my mother driving Sally and me through the winter dark and through patches of cold mist to his birthday party.

When my mother and Sally and I disembarked and waded through the waves of mist, Edmund and his father came out of the house to meet us. Mr Waller invited Sally and then me to peer through a glass porthole no larger than a small roll of Scotch tape in the left of the two grey stone gateposts.

We found ourselves looking into a little brightly lit room inside the post. It was decorated, furnished like a room in a doll's house, with two children in it, the boy fair-haired like Edmund, two adults . . .

Was this a scene from a folk-tale? Or purely imaginary? Or were the Waller family holding themselves up to the light? I was fascinated, and I remember stealing out of the house when the party was in full swing to have another long look. In a poem for children, I noted that this 'world inside the world' lacked any changing tide, and that uncertainty and flux are preconditions of beauty:

> . . . I want change, I want choice:
> the unpredictable throw of the dice,
> the fluctuating human voice,
> and sweet and sour, and hot and cold.
> Whatever the price,
> give me this unfinished world.*

At Whiteleaf my parents devised and did the legwork for a series of stupendous birthday parties for Sally and me. Some were treasure hunts, some were paperchases, and they all took place over an extended area and were designed to ensure their participants returned muddy, well exercised, with specimens to show and tales to tell, just in time for tea in the fading light.

The centrepiece of these birthday teas was a cake pieced together by my mother with infinite care during the preceding days. Her masterpiece was an enormous battleship, complete with gun turrets and the like, all of it iced sombre blue-grey.

I was never enamoured of war-toys, though so much of our play, I realise, was about war – time-bombs, bases, cowboys and Indians – and during the war the whole Vale of Aylesbury had been peppered with airfields at Booker and Halton, Haddenham and Cheddington and Thame; but my war-cake was the envy of boys for miles around, and everyone took home an extra helping of it neatly wrapped in a paper serviette.

The impact of these birthday parties has lasted all my life. I've organised the same sort of chases for my own children, and invited adults to treasure hunts. Quite often, as a writer, I have used an object, such as a key or an old bone comb, as the cornerstone for a story, and at one party I asked my guests to bring back an ancient object, and tell us all a convincing story about it – a mission triumphantly achieved by one well-known

* From 'The World Inside the World'.

poet who returned from the banks of the Thames at Greenwich, as scruffy as a twelve-year-old, with what may or may not have been a Roman tile.

What parties! The years pass, and over and over again, one image reassembles itself, unbidden.

It is my twelfth birthday, and my treasure-hunt partner Ann and I are standing in an utterly silent beechwood. Around us, there are lean, smooth, grey-green torsos. Under our feet, the ground is springy with mast, dead leaves, twigs. Over our heads, the arms and fingers of the trees reach out and interlock.

We have come this far, following scraps of red rag tied by my parents to low branches, arrows chalked on the tree trunks.

This far was easy enough, but where now? Where next? Have we missed a sign? And where is everyone else?

In the Beechwoods

At weekends, home from London, my father often took Sally and me for long walks in the beechwoods.

Together, we springheeled down King's Street, a green nave flickering with light, a hollow road layered with fallen leaves that is mentioned in the Monks Risborough charter of AD 903. And there we speculated about who the king might have been, and first learned the useful mnemonic, 'Willie, Willie, Harry, Ste, Harry, Dick, John, Harry 3', and so on. I remember thinking our king must have had a huge army of followers to wear the track down until it was actually sunken.

Each year my father paid a fee of £1 to the Hampden Estate for the privilege of bringing home as much firewood as he could carry, an arrangement that had a feudal ring to it.

Time and again, Sally and I – sometimes in tandem – dragged huge branches down the hill, and once straight down the middle of the Cross. To begin with, the challenge was its own reward; but sometimes the branches were heavy, slimy and fungus-ridden, and then it was as much as we could do to cart them home.

In the little wooden lean-to behind our cottage, my father kept a saw and sawing-block, and an axe. First we helped him to snap off the dead twigs for kindling; and then he sawed the

The Bodgers' work-site in the Chilterns (1905)

branches and split them, and his face turned pink and shiny. I helped him to stack the logs against one side of the cottage until they almost reached up to the eaves, like an Alpine chalet.

Sometimes, I asked my parents whether we could try to find the bodger*– a man living rough in the high woods, fashioning beech furniture. I realise now that they plainly had no idea where he was to be found, but somehow they managed to make a mystery out of it, and to convince us that this wodwo would only show himself when he chose to do so. Of course, the more often we searched for him, the larger he loomed in our imaginations, until his absence was as his presence:

> *You can see he made this table. Now feel*
> *this kitchen chair. He makes chests and what-nots*
> *and stools and stands. No two are alike*
> *and they belong like a family –*
> Yes, I remember my mother's words:
> *He's the man to follow if only you can find him.*

* Bodgers worked with green wood that split and twisted as it dried out; hence, bodged work. There has long been a tradition of furniture-making in and around High Wycombe (as well as the manufacture of brooms, wooden skewers and lacemakers' bobbins).

I'll follow the arrow chalked on this trunk
to a glade gone quiet in the midday heat,
a branch so low I swing on it, the skirts
of my climbing tree. The wild boys
held their councils right underneath me.
I could fight them with my feet.

And King's Street now, bouncy with leaf mould
and beech twigs and mast: no-one knows
who the king was – a matted beard,
a wooden mask. It's always raining here.
Walking back to this green dripping
gloom, I am unborn again.

The '14–'18 ditches, and tangled raspberry
canes, and the Neolithic mound; this is where
Christine and I played sardines in pairs,
and it was much too late when we were found.
High on this hill, half the world at my feet,
I hear my mother's Alpine bell ringing.

Tell me more about the bodger!
He picks and fells his beeches single-handed,
and they never have fewer
than fifty rings. He seasons them
with sunlight and rain and rime and birdsong.
He's the green man, all right.

As far as she knew he lived on his own
in the middle of the woods. *Listen for his lathe!*
Time and time again with this clean sheet,
this loaded pen, I've come back
listening for him. And I still
think I'll run him to earth.*

    As a boy, I thought of the beechwoods and hills simply as
'the woods', but now I know their names, some practical,

* *New and Selected Poems 1965 – 1990:* 'The Bodger'

some secretive and suggestive. Giles Wood, Sergeant's Wood, Hillock Wood. But also Ninn Wood and Hobb's Hill and Cymbeline's Mount, in some way associated with Cunobelin, leader of the Catevellauni and the most powerful Briton in the south of England during the first four decades of the first century AD. 'Radiant Cymbeline', Shakespeare called him.

I know, too, the paintings and drawings of John Nash who, better than anyone, catches the hidden and graceful, billowing, somehow fluid and feminine nature of the beechwoods; I know Clare Leighton's miraculous wood-engravings, so solid yet so delicate, so minutely observant. And I'm aware that Gilbert White wrote that 'The beech is the most lovely of all forest trees.'

Bringing us up on her own throughout the week, our mother must have been glad to get us out of her hair, and on our long, often memorable walks, my father always encouraged us to be aware of the numinous. Whether or not the otherworld was for him an actuality or a metaphor I'm not entirely sure, but either way it was more constantly present than in any other highly educated adult I've known.

Once, when we were standing on top of Whiteleaf Hill and looking west over the Vale of Aylesbury, I asked him how far we could see. How many miles.

As usual, my father was in no hurry to answer. After a while, he said, 'Well, as far as Oxford . . . the Cotswolds. As far as Wales, do you think?'

Immense as the view is, this was completely impossible, and of course he knew as much.

'Can you really?' I asked. 'How far is it?'

'Well,' said my father gently, eyes closed. 'If you close your eyes and open your eyes, you may be able to. On a clear day.'

And in a way, he was right of course. It all depends on how you look at it.

My father's way of educating Sally and me was not so much to tell as to point, to guide and then give us the space to find out for ourselves.

When I was six, and we were sitting on the hilltop, my father told me a story – and it was one that, at my insistence, he repeated many times over the following years. I never tired of hearing it any more than I tired of hearing my grandmother's accounts of scenes from my father's and uncle's childhood.

There was a king, said my father, a Welsh king. Far from home, he was very badly wounded in a battle against the English. But he did not die, and neither did his stricken followers. They went into a hill, they went under a hill, and there in a great stone chamber they lie asleep. They sleep and wait until the day when they'll come out of the cave, and drive all the English – all the descendants of the Angles and Saxons and Frisians and Jutes – back into the cold North Sea across which they first came.

I was enthralled. And I didn't doubt for one moment that the hill beneath which King Arthur lay asleep was Whiteleaf Cross.

Accordingly, I devoted a fair amount of time to trying to find the entrance to the passageway leading to the stone chamber. In the chalkpit on one side of the hill, there were fissures; near the First World War practice trenches, there was a strange circular hollow; there was one old oak with a trunk so large you could step inside it. And what about the huge, dark-green water tank deep in the woods, with fencing and a plunging ditch around it? Was it really just a water tank, or was there more to it than that?

Biting Mrs Robertson

Aged three, I'm standing on the threshold of my first school, a nursery school in Wilmslow, near Manchester. My teacher is Mrs Robertson.

Now I can see a full-sized, long-legged oblong table, occupying most of the room's floorspace, and we're all sitting around it, though how this is possible unless we're on built-up chairs or stacks of cushions, I have no idea. I can see myself sliding off my chair under the table, and hoping Mrs Robertson won't notice. I'm crawling around on all fours under the table. And I can still feel Mrs Robertson jerk and hear her loud yelp when I sink my teeth into the calf of her right leg.

Later, my parents gave me a beautiful rocking-horse, covered with real horse-hide and horsehair, and I called it Mrs Robertson. I wrote her name in capital letters on the underside of the main strut, though whether this was an act of exculpation or continuing adoration, I don't know.

And that, I fear, is all I remember about my first school.

I was four when we returned to the Chilterns after the war, and at once my mother took me for an interview with Mrs Rene Howden, a woman scarcely less substantial and strong-willed than my mother, who ran a nursery school in a cottage named after the beautiful sumach tree standing in front of it. This was in the neighbouring village of Askett.

I had to climb a little ladder and pop out through a hatch on the first floor to meet my interviewer.

'Do you know the three Rs?' she asked me.

'Yes.'

As soon as we were safely back home, I asked my mother what the three Rs were.

Nevertheless, Mrs Howden found a place for me, and of this first year at Sumach Cottage School I have two memories.

The first is of one of the teachers, Mrs Boulting – one of the film-making family with whom I've crossed paths several times, never with any great pleasure. Seeing me reluctant to come into school at the beginning of my second week, Mrs Boulting grabbed hold of my right ear.

'It's all right,' she told my mother. 'I'll take him in.'

With that, my mother drove off, and Mrs Boulting pulled me all the way down the drive into the school by the right ear, like a prize beast at a county show – in my case, a very nervous calf. I'm perfectly aware my mother regarded a teacher as *in loco parentis* and took the view that a little physical pressure never did any harm, but the way in which she so cheerfully abandoned me still irks me!

In the classroom at the top of the ladder, I see myself sitting in the back row but one, and I don't know what to write or draw. I keep looking over the shoulder of the girl in front of me and trying to see her work. I want to steal her ideas. I know I shouldn't be doing this. I know I am cheating. To my mother, cheating was anathema, and I still feel uncomfortable when I remember this small scene, probably all the more so because I wasn't caught and ticked off.

Since then, I've twice been involved in cheating episodes – the first was with my blameless friend Antony, when we were sixteen. I offered to help him with a Latin translation that I'd already completed and handed in, and my memory was all too good. Mr Griffin was presented with two virtually identical translations. For heaven knows how long, the three of us stumped up and down the school's immense central corridor, and Antony and I were subjected to an intense grilling. I remember feeling rather elated at being in the soup with him; he, conversely, felt tainted. His eyes blazed, then brimmed. We were given a conditional discharge. It was a crisis that cemented our friendship.

The second occasion was while I was invigilating at a Bavarian university. When I routinely asked well over two hundred students to show their ID cards, there was a great kerfuffle. Virtually half of them were taking the exam on behalf of their friends, and they all stood up and walked out. Even now, when I watch sport and see professional fouls and play-acting, I feel quite immoderate and angry about it.

From Everlasting to Everlasting

I have inherited a Russian Orthodox incense burner, made of gold-painted tin and inlaid with circles of cut glass – burgundy and cerulean and moss and amber. My grandfather Frank brought it back from a trip (probably a scientific mission) to pre-Revolutionary Saint Petersburg in 1908 during which, switching from the Julian to the Gregorian calendar, he arrived five days before he left. Looking at this garish object now, I realise how anyone who visited Crosskeys without already knowing its occupants would have seen signs everywhere of my parents' attention to the inner life but been perplexed about the precise nature of their religious persuasions.

My mother and father were both brought up as Church of England communicants. They were married in church and they both had Christian funerals and are buried, as they wished, in hallowed ground. But both undertook sustained religious quests far removed from any Christian orthodoxy.

My mother's instinctive approach to religion was straightforward and well earthed. It was through her fingertips, though it was never muscular and never crassly literalist. Humans are apt to create deities in their own image – that's to say as humans writ large, like giant shadows cast by flickering firelight on a presiding wall – and in her twenties, my mother would really have liked her God to be amiable, tennis-playing, pipe-smoking, with a sense of humour.

My father's approach, on the other hand, was contemplative and mystical. He believed that, of its nature, spiritual truth could only be arrived at after study and through meditation, and was literally inexpressible. When I was quite young, he told me about the many names given to God as masks for his true name, this as opposed to the myriad names that simply indicate how many human spokes there are in God's Wheel.

My father's quest was crucial to his life as a composer and musicologist; and because she loved him and, loving him, wanted to share his dreams, my mother went with him to an arcane society that met weekly to study the writings of Ouspensky.

But maybe there was an additional reason. After we returned from the north to Crosskeys, my father found a job in the Music Department of the BBC, and he elected to live all week in 'digs' in London, and came home only at the weekend.

I doubt whether Sally and I ever heard our parents criticise each other during our entire childhood, but I understood my mother didn't like my father's absences, and I think that after a while she became suspicious of them. So her Wednesday trips to London punctuated the long week and maybe enabled her to check up on him if not to keep him in check.

On the cottage shelves were the works of medieval mystics, such as *The Cloud of Unknowing*, and later writers such as William Blake and Thomas Traherne and Richard Jefferies.

I remember listening to a radio performance of Gerald Finzi's *Dies Natalis* with my father when I was eleven or twelve. He put on the table in front of me Traherne's burning words:

I was a stranger, which at my entrance into the world was saluted and surrounded with innumerable joys; my knowledge was Divine . . . Certainly Adam in Paradise had not more sweet and curious apprehensions of the world than I . . . The corn was orient and immortal wheat, which never should be reap'd nor was ever sown. I thought it had stood from everlasting to everlasting.*

Although I didn't fully comprehend them, these words scorched me. They branded me. I knew then there are truths deeper than logic or understanding, deeper than words, and my father knew that I knew.

Next to the medieval and later mystical writers stood books on Buddhism and Vedanta, arcane philosophical treatises without lettering on their spines or informative title-pages, the writings of Gurdjieff and Ouspensky, handwritten booklets. On one wall hung a Tibetan mandala, on ledges lay an assortment of oriental musical instruments, including a Tibetan skull-drum and thigh-bone oboe, and at the top of the staircase sat my father's very beautiful, ancient marble Buddha. There he was, arms crossed, legs crossed, always smiling and unsmiling, somehow neither unmoved nor unduly moved by the bustle around him.

I often knelt on the stairs, and gazed at the Buddha gazing at me, but I never presumed to talk to him as I did to my teddy bear and my golliwog and my lead soldiers.

Even now, scarcely a day passes without my thinking about him. I've seen him sitting in a little orange-and-lemon grove in Sylmar in California, and sitting in a hill-house overlooking the River Teifi in Wales, and continue to hope that, for the next leg in his wide wandering, he may come here to North Norfolk. In him, matter and spirit are so perfectly reconciled.

When I was seven or eight, I was taken, and I have no idea why, to meet the leaders of the arcane Wednesday society, known nondescriptly but rather impressively as 'The Work'.

In Harley Street, I sat surrounded by my parents and three or four suited men. It was as if I were attending the first of my

* Finzi's free adaptation of the opening of Traherne's *Third Century of Meditations*.

life's many interviews, and maybe I was. But why? And for what?

In one occasional friend, my father's and mother's worlds were wonderfully reconciled. This was the great Swiss explorer, sportswoman and philosopher, Ella Maillart. My parents had met her several times in London and then went to see her in the very high Alpine village of Chandolin in the Valais.

Ella had skied and sailed for Switzerland in the 1924 Olympics; with Peter Fleming, Ian's brother, she pioneered the route across Northern Tibet she describes in *Forbidden Journey*; she practised and taught Vedanta, and had an Indian guru.

My parents' admiration for Ella impressed itself mightily on me. Much later, when I was an Oxford student, reading English and thinking of studying for the priesthood, I followed in their footsteps to Chandolin. With me came my diffident and brilliant friend John Gurney, later Fellow in Persian and Islamic Studies at Wadham College, Oxford.

As the dew fell, we set up our little tent. John was all for our establishing ourselves in Chandolin for a day or two before introducing ourselves to Ella; and with my usual impetuosity, I was all for descending on her at once for a night-cap. I had my way.

The next day, I asked Ella about Vedanta. Seeing at once how impressionable I was, and how muddled my thinking, she promptly rerouted my questions and encouraged me to be a better Christian.

'It's difficult enough,' she said, 'to practise your own culture's faith, let alone the faith of another culture. You shouldn't consider Vedanta or Buddhism or anything else unless you really cannot make further headway with Christianity.'

Over coffee one morning, I asked Ella some question I thought to be deeply meaningful.

Ella looked at me – this eager, bright-eyed acolyte with his gentle, thinking friend.

'Sit up!' she commanded me.

'What?'

'Sit up! You're not allowing enough blood to flow to your head. And if you don't do that, what hope have you got of really understanding anything? Sit up straight!'

John and I went walking and scrambling, sometimes together, sometimes alone. I took a path that led me through sweet-smelling Arolla pines, and the ground bounced underfoot. Then I emerged on to a field, it was scarcely more than that . . .

Despite sporadic attempts, I am not at all skilled at meditation. But when I try to empty and pacify my mind, one image often resurfaces, and has done so for almost fifty years, the image of that field, strewn with so many wildflowers and grasses, gently nodding and shaking, perched four thousand feet above the blue-green floor of the Valais.

I remember those charmed days in Chandolin so vividly that I must have lived them with great intensity and great attention to the specific.

When I was ten, stimulated by my parents' quests and not disaffected by daily doses of chapel at school, I began to grow more interested in religion. My parents encouraged me but at the same time suggested that no one faith can have a monopoly of the truth.

They argued that while Christian missionary work had undoubted social value, it had also caused strife and that in any case it was arrogant and wrong to preach the superiority of the Christian faith.

'Truth is not like that, is it?' my father asked me. 'The faiths of the world are like the faces of a many-sided pyramid. Where do they all meet?'

The Invisible Worm

My grandmother, Mary, lost no fewer than seven children before giving birth to my mother.

'My mother didn't want me,' my mother told Sally in her old age. 'She went away.'

'No,' Sally replied. 'As you've told me before, she went away to a sanatorium in Switzerland because she was ill. She did want you.'

Even though I know it well, I still find Hans Andersen's shocking farmyard scene in *The Ugly Duckling* difficult to take. To begin with, the mother duck defends her baby when the other ducks round on him and the old duck with Spanish blood disparages him; the way in which the ugly duckling is reviled by his siblings is bad enough, but when his mother in desperation and sorrow can no longer stand by him, I feel unutterably sad.

'I wish you weren't here,' she says. 'I wish you were a long way away.'

When I was thirteen and Sally was ten, we went to the Three Choirs Festival in Worcester Cathedral for a performance of one of my father's most beautiful pieces, his cantata *The*

Sacred Dance, coupled with the first performance of Ralph Vaughan Williams's great oratorio, *Hodie*. There the great composer sat Sally on his knee and told her that, if ever our parents tired of her, he would adopt her.

This idea was as risible as it was meant to be. Though neither of them felt the need to tell us and the ways in which they manifested it could scarcely have been more unalike, we took our parents' love for granted.

In so far as I thought about it all, I also supposed that their marriage was on an even keel. That is what they wanted Sally and me to believe. In the garden of our early childhood, we were unaware of the invisible worm.

How blind I was. Did I partly choose to be? And is it better that I was?

> 'Well, well, go & play till the light fades away
> And then go home to bed.'
> The little ones leaped and shouted and laugh'd
> And all the hills ecchoed.*

In the garden of my early childhood, yes, in the night-garden . . . I am standing alone.

Out of our cottage and down the short path come two men carrying a stretcher, and my mother is lying on it, white-faced, eyes closed, covered in a scarlet blanket.

I know I will never see her again, and no one thinks to tell me otherwise.

My father must have reassured me, the ambulance-men must have said something, but what I remember is my pain, and how completely lost I felt after she had gone.

How old was I when my mother had this miscarriage? Four, I think. It doesn't really matter. I stood alone by the gate for minutes that time's interest has increased to hours. I stared through the door into the dark.

That is what my mother also did when she discovered that

* William Blake, from *Songs of Innocence*: 'Nurse's Song'.

she was pregnant for the third time. Her marriage was troubled and, as I've recently learned from Sally, she decided she couldn't face having another child. She talked to her doctor-father about this, and he gave her an injection that may have led later to her losing her baby.

As an only child, my mother experienced none of the early rough-and-tumble shared by brothers and sisters or, to use one of the more unpleasant words in the English language, siblings. Add to this a disciplined, no-nonsense mother with a middle-class distaste for showing physical affection, and it's plain that she had no model for bringing up her own children.

In the event, her balancing act between rule and rebellious instinct, reason and powerful, suppressed sensuality, was one that preoccupied her all her life.

Articulate as she was, my mother's way of expressing feeling was not with word but action; her response to a setback was to take it on the chin, uncomplaining, and to regard it as a challenge. Her way of coping with loss, so much at odds with today's sensibility, was to internalise it, say as little about it as possible, and press on. This doesn't mean she didn't feel pain; she certainly did, but to her mind this didn't justify inflicting it on others.

Whatever the truth about being wanted or unwanted, my mother certainly related more strongly to her father than to her mother. There is a good photograph of my grandfather Claude sucking a pipe and looking mildly amused at life. Not to disengage but, rather, to accept life's slings and arrows; not to take oneself too seriously, and to keep a sense of proportion; not overly to philosophise: these were some of the attitudes my mother inherited from him.

Not long after my grandmother Mary died an excruciatingly painful death of cancer (only a few months before my mother married), Grandpa Claude married Irene, the nurse at his practice in Leighton Buzzard who was only one year older than my mother, and they had a son, Clive. In 1948, the three of them went on an extended holiday to South Africa.

They rented a house near Pretoria, but they hadn't been

there long before Clive, aged six, strayed down to their swimming pool and fell in. No one heard his cries; he drowned. My grandfather and Irene then decided to prolong their stay – in similar circumstances, I imagine I'd do the same.

Not long after this, Irene wrote to say that she had gone into the bedroom and found a cobra there, and that she had listened, terrified, while the servants beat it to death. And then, early on the morning of 29 January 1950, I was sitting on my parents' bed at Crosskeys when there was a knock at the door: a telegram for my mother. My father brought it up to her in bed, and I remember my mother's sharp intake of breath. 'Daddy's dead!' she said.* Then she covered her mouth and nose with one hand. My father at once gently ushered me out of the bedroom into my own room, across the top of the stairs.

Covering . . . ushering . . . Grief was not something to be vented, like the wonderful, terrible keening I heard once on the remote Irish island of Tory, and certainly not anything to be shared with young children.

When I was nine, I heard sobbing in my father's study. Cautiously, I put my head round the door, and there was my mother, who thought she was alone in the house, sitting on a stool by the dead ashes in the grate, crying her eyes out. I was shocked and very concerned. Then she saw me and gathered me to her. I'd never seen my mother cry before, and I never did again.

Maybe she was remembering her father, or her mother, or Clive, whose loss was as difficult to take as that of any child; maybe she had come across something in my father's study that set alarm bells ringing; maybe the cause of her tears was less specific – *sunt lacrimae rerum*.

No matter what, I see now that my mother's natural high spirits though not her resolve were already being eroded: not by the sacrifice of her life as a potter but by my father's

* Claude Marriott Lovell Cowper died in Cape Town of a heart attack. He was seventy. His body was brought back to England, and he is buried in West Wittering in Sussex.

inability to return her love in equal measure, by his week-long absences, and by money worries. My father's BBC salary was limited and my mother's share in her father's estate was to be held in trust until the death of her young stepmother.

In 1948, after what seems to have been a quite rigorous selection process, my mother had already taken on freelance work, conducting social surveys. This entailed driving around a designated area, knocking on the doors of complete strangers, and persuading them to answer a large number of questions about the way they lived their lives.

This work meant that she could at least get Sally and me off to school in the morning even if she couldn't always be there when we got home. Sometimes we were farmed out to friends for an hour or two, and sometimes we caught the regular bus service that ran from Little Kimble to Monks Risborough, where we were met by May Phillips.

May was the buxom daughter of the family who had farmed the high pastures at Green Hailey since at least the turn of the century, and she was my mother's cleaner and our carer. Why do I remember our afternoon slog up steep Peter's Lane to high Whiteleaf, and on up to our cottage at the top of the village, with such fondness? In part because of the easy, unselfconscious affection May bestowed on Sally and me.

We left in our wake Mrs Carwithen's house, and the sounds of piano-playing within; we climbed past the house of Clare Leighton, author and illustrator of *Four Hedges* and *The Garden* – hers is the image of Whiteleaf Cross that I'm most fond of, while I also have a copy of her engraving *A Lapful of Windfalls* (see opposite) that makes my heart miss a beat every time I look at it; we peered into the deep soakaway, down into the chalky grey-green water, and poked and prodded it with little sticks; yes, it was always summer.

After some time, May was courted by a young farmer called Frank. Sally and I had no objection to that. But then May told us that Frank lived far away in Wiltshire and that, when she married him, she would leave Green Hailey Farm and go and live in Wiltshire as well. This was an entirely different matter.

When I was eighteen, and just beginning to write poems, I remembered my green jealousy with these very simple, bitter-sweet verses:

'Those apples, like temptations, like feelings, like words . . .': *A Lapful of Windfalls*: wood engraving by Clare Leighton

May strode down from her father's farm,
At her throat there dangled a charm
The man she loved had given her.
And he was the son of a farmer.
                              But I loved May.

I was six and my sister three,
May's daily liability
Until at dusk she walked back home,
Milked the Jerseys and dreamed alone.
                              How I loved May.

Once she told me: Post this letter.
May, you should have chosen better!
I saw that demon farmer's name
And fibbed I'd lost the note in the lane.
                              For I loved May.

May turned maroon, dealt me a snorter
Worthy of a farmer's daughter.
And she came no more. I meant you no harm,
And for all that you still have your charm,
                              My dear May.

And what did I do with the letter? I slid it out across the
brimming soakaway, and then I pushed it down and held it
under with a stick.

While I was away at school, Sally was a bridesmaid at May's
wedding and some years later, my mother drove us both to
Wiltshire to see her and her growing family. I remember how
secretly apprehensive I was about meeting Frank, and how I
was quite sure that May knew exactly what I had done.

Sublimations, submergings, drownings . . .

Grandpa Frank and Neenie

My father's parents, Frank and Irene Crossley-Holland, lived at the panelled neo-Elizabethan mansion of Oakwell Park near Soulbury in Bedfordshire. Above the hall there was an organ gallery, and there my grandfather sat, short-legged and cigar-smoking, playing Victorian hymns.

The third and last child of Manoah and Kezia Holland, my grandfather was an altogether remarkable polymath who never suffered fools gladly and was an authoritarian *pater familias*. Born in 1878, he stood five foot eight inches tall 'in his socks', had grey eyes, and black hair cut short and parted near the centre. My father described how he bridled at his father's attempts to determine his career, and I suspect that his own relatively early marriage, at the age of twenty-three, may have partly been due to a desire to make his own way in life.

My grandfather was firstly a pharmacist. He invented Iodex in 1910, and this provided the family with a limited income until the 1970s, when our small continuing interest was bought out by Smith, Kline and French. He wrote *The Pharmacy Handbook* (1914) and served as Chairman of the British Pharmaceutical Conference in 1935.

Called to the Bar in 1918, Grandpa Frank also stood for parliament as a liberal in 1922 in the Hemsworth constituency in Yorkshire. Lloyd George sent him a telegram beginning:

> Your scientific attainments and brilliant research work entitle you to special consideration at the hands of the electors of Hemsworth in the rebuilding of British Trade and industries. Men of your expert knowledge are urgently required in the House of Commons.

After the first count, my grandfather was prematurely announced as the winner; there was a recount, though, and he lost. The local paper praised him for his wit, resource and fight.

As a little boy, I simplified my paternal grandmother's name from Irene to Neenie, and that's what our side of the family called her.

I adored my grandmother. She loved her sons, Peter and Dick; and after them, she loved me, and often told me as much. She was uncomplicated and unselfconscious and forbearing and kind. Her greatest pleasure was to please others.

Neenie was born in 1884, seventh and last child of Alexander Charles Dickins and Elizabeth (née Green). Only recently I discovered that when Grandpa Frank asked Neenie's father for his permission to marry her, Mr Dickins imposed an unexpected condition. It was that their firstborn son (my father, that's to say) should be circumcised. This was at the insistence of his wife Elizabeth, whose father Abraham Green was Jewish. Apparently, Grandpa Frank was nettled but in any case he accepted it, and he and my pretty, petite grandmother were married in Bridlington in 1911.

According to my father, Grandpa Frank was worried that if it became known he had married a woman who was part-Jewish, part-Gentile, it might jeopardise his career and so he made Neenie promise never to mention it. One would certainly never have guessed as much from her appearance. She was quite pale-skinned, with quiet blue eyes and auburn hair.

Devoted and by nature submissive, Neenie kept her promise,

and it wasn't until shortly before she died in her nineties that she told my father. Despite knowing my own interest in the family's genealogy, however, my father died without choosing to tell me.

Grandpa Frank was decidedly and even definingly interested in his family's genealogy. Oakwell Park was decorated not only with shields bearing the Holland coat-of-arms (to which he was entitled) but also those of the Black Prince, who married Joan Holland, the Fair Maid of Kent, and Richard II, their son.

Since the age of seventeen, he had reinforced the surname Holland by preceding it with his mother's maiden name, Crossley. And when he was appointed High Sheriff of Bedfordshire in 1939, he formalised this, changing his name to Crossley-Holland by deed poll, as well as submitting to the College of Heralds for a new grant of arms.

Frank the son of Manoah (a Methodist priest) and his second wife Kezia, the son of Absalom and Sarah (née Tansey), the son of Peter and Jane (née Burrows) . . .

In 1939, my grandfather was granted and assigned arms:

> Per chevron Azure semée dy Lys Argent and Vert in chief two Lions rampant of the second and in base a cross Tau and two crosses Moline Or . . . to be borne and used for ever hereafter by him the said Frank William Crossley-Holland and by his descendants with due and proper differences according to the law of Arms.

My grandfather devised a new Latin motto for the family: *Ut possim more maiorum* – That I may do according to the manner of my ancestors. This certainly begs more questions than it answers, but anyhow points to a respect for continuity.

I have in turn written this memoir in the same spirit:

> I call on those that call me son,
> Grandson, or great-grandson,
> On uncles, aunts, great-uncles or great-aunts,
> To judge what I have done.*

* W. B. Yeats: from 'Are You Content?'

Switzerland

Winterfreuden im sonnigen Hochgebirge der Schweiz, announces the postcard, while the magical, somewhat Chagall-like painting depicts two daring woolly-hatted skiers cutting elegant curves through shadow and sunlight.

Another card, dated 1923, shows a splendid, low-slung, open-topped, yellow Alpine bus, packed with well-kitted passengers, one with a scarf flying à la Isadora Duncan, crossing a bridge over a dashing mountain torrent flanked by gentians.

And a third, 1928 this one, portrays a pipe-smoking man on his haunches, tightening one of his companion's ski-straps. She is wearing plus fours, with a patterned top and elegant hat to match it, and smiling gaily. Behind them rises the Jungfrau . . . and below them lies elegant sepia lettering, *'Wengen Oberland Bernois'.*

The painters, designers and promoters of these and similar cards didn't miss a trick. Effective in promoting tourism and often strikingly well painted, they bear witness to the way in which the nineteenth-century English love affair with the Alps was developed by the Swiss after the end of the First World War into a full-blown, year-round tourist industry.

During her teens and early twenties, my mother went skiing

L'ÉTÉ en SUISSE

PUBLIÉ PAR L'OFFICE SUISSE DU TOURISME, ZURICH ET LAUSANNE

WOLFSBERG ZURICH

in Switzerland every winter, first with her parents, then with friends. The places she loved above all were Mürren and Wengen in the Bernese Oberland.

So it was entirely natural that, as England started to shrug off its siege-mentality after six years at war, and people began to move about freely, even to take holidays, my mother's thoughts should turn to Switzerland. Her first choice would have been to go skiing with my father but, as he was not in the least interested in winter sports, and seldom supportive of her pleasures, a summer holiday it had to be.

'*L'ÉTÉ en SUISSE*', another card announces. And as it had

to be a summer holiday, my parents decided to take my grand-mother Neenie and me with them.

So far as I know, my mother and father, wedded in September 1939, never had even one holiday on their own except for their honeymoon in the Cotswolds. I keep walking round their marriage, puzzling over what went wrong and when, and then wondering in which ways the failure of their marriage may have coloured Sally's and my lives. One aspect of adulthood is to seek to understand and not to blame; another is to take full responsibility for one's own actions. I had to live through my own very turbulent twenties and thirties before I recognised that.

Aged three, Sally was left at home in the care of my mother's best friend, Mary Shaw, at whose wartime wedding I had been a page. My parents, Neenie and I drove in our trusty Morris 10 to London Airport, at Northolt.

The first days of our holiday were spent on the Lake of Lucerne. This enabled my father to visit Richard and Cosima Wagner's idyllic retreat on the islet of Triebschen.

My mother's feeling for classical music, let alone the music of a Jew-hating German, was almost as limited as my father's for winter sports, and so my father took me over to Triebschen. In a pedal-boat!

Within a couple of minutes, my right foot somehow got jammed in my pedal and I twisted my ankle.

I howled! How I howled, and on the landing-stage my mother kept calling out and beckoning. But my father wasn't to be deflected from his quest. Once he had disengaged my foot, and pacified me, we pressed on.

We can all connect some pieces of music with specific places, but altogether fewer with where they were actually composed. I've sat on Bredon Hill and sung out Vaughan Williams, and prowled the North Norfolk saltmarshes with the slow movement of Moeran's Symphony in G minor in my ears, and I've skulked in the shadows of Notre-Dame with Pérotin, but none of these were as memorable as the painful pleasure of

Triebschen where Wagner composed his sublime *Siegfried Idyll*, and a chamber orchestra of thirteen players, assembled on the staircase, serenaded Cosima with its first performance as she woke on her birthday in 1870.

From Lucerne, we travelled by train to Interlaken, and then Lauterbrunnen, and from there took the rack-and-pinion train to Wengen. I don't remember anything of the thrill of seeing the Jungfrau, the Eiger and the Mönch for the first time, though I have a little black-and-white snapshot in which my father, and Neenie wearing a floral dress, and I, wearing sensible grey shorts down to my knees and hands clasped as if in prayer, are standing in front of them. What I recall is how much Neenie and I, sixty and six, loved one another's company. While my parents went on much longer and more ambitious hikes, she and I went strolling round the traffic-free village, buying small treats (walking-stick badges, little squares of Frigor chocolate), and swimming in the breathtakingly cold open-air swimming pool.

Once, we caught the rattling mountain train up to Kleine Scheidegg. En route, we paused in the middle of a high meadow. The sun looked in through the open window. Then two faces peered in – my mother and father! Their fists were full of wildflowers, they were laughing, we were laughing, meeting by chance before meeting by design at high Kleine Scheidegg, beneath the dark, smoking north face of the Eiger.

Now, of course, it's illegal to pick the rarer wildflowers and socially unacceptable to bring down much more than a daisy, but when I was six, each table in the dining room of the Belvedere Hotel was decorated with that day's already-drooping pickings.

I thought of this when I returned to Wengen a couple of years ago, and put simple words for children into the Eiger's (i.e. the Ogre's) mouth. At the back of my mind, too, was haunting Blodeuedd, the woman in the *Mabinogion* made of flowers:

49

But I am made of flowers also.
I have golden ox-eyes
And bears'-ears, fleshy.
My lips are cow's lips
And I grow a mauve beard
With five points.

The tube of my throat is freezing indigo.

I creep, I shrithe
on my devil's claws,
and sting whatever I touch.

All my wives are toothed and scaly,
they shake their heads.
Melancholy thistles!

Look! The dwarf bells
are my nodding servants.

In summer
I am made of flowers.

Each evening, I ate on my own at six o'clock in the hotel's grand, damasked dining room, and each evening the same pinafored waitress served me. Then she took me up to my room, got me into my pyjamas, watched over me while I brushed my teeth, tucked me up, and kissed me goodnight – all this while my parents and grandmother were doubtless having a short stroll and pre-prandial drinks downstairs.

It was a perfectly satisfactory arrangement, in accord with a time when middle-class mothers felt no need to mollycoddle their offspring. I fell passionately in love with my waitress and spent some of my pocket-money on an unlined exercise book.

On the title page is the proclamation *I LOVE THE WATRIS*, and each page of the book repeats some or all of these words in red crayon, bold and erratic, surrounded by sprightly, skipping musical notes.

So this was my first, my most unequivocal and joyous book!

From the age of twelve onward, I went back to Switzerland many times, and on several occasions to Wengen, where Sally and I were so enamoured of the plump duvets that night by night we alternated, sleeping either with both duvets on one bed, or with neither. I took my mother to Wengen for what we both knew would be her last visit, and we witnessed the transhumance – the dramatic procession of garlanded cattle from their winter quarters to the lush mountain pastures, led by the farmer himself, repeatedly singing out 'hop-hop-hop'. We rode on the train astoundingly cut through the Eiger up to the dazzling Jungfraujoch, and ate raclette, and swung on the long cable-car ride down towards Grindelwald. The first time that we had done this, riding in tandem when I was six, I petrified my mother by swinging back the protective bar and exclaiming, 'Look! It opens!'

'Now,' my mother said, 'we take electricity for granted. But when we came here in 1947, out of grey, ration-book Britain, it was the bright lights everywhere that were so different. It felt like coming out of a prison into a fairground.'

One day my mother told me she wanted to get over to Adelboden.

'That's where I went skiing for the last time,' she said. 'Not that I knew it would be. I left my skis there.'

At the grand 125-room Nevada Palace Hotel, where American airmen who survived crash-landings in Switzerland had been interned during the war, my mother marched up to the receptionist.

'Bonjour!' she said. 'I stayed here in 1937, and I left my skis here.'

Before long, an ancient caretaker still in the service of the hotel slowly hobbled across the reception area.

In a mixture of English and French, my mother explained her quest and the caretaker, plainly well used to strong-minded Englishwomen, invited her to come up with him 'en haut'.

'To the attic,' the receptionist explained.

'I think I'll need a chaperone,' my mother said quite primly.

She turned to me, 'You'd better come with me.'

I could scarcely believe my eyes. In the spotless attic seven stories up stood a row of smooth brown leather suitcases and pairs of skis, each labelled with the name of its English owner.

As it happens, my mother's skis were not amongst them, but for quite some time we inspected the labels and, making out the names of not only the Misses but the Majors and Captains, saw in that quiet place an emblem of high hopes dashed and death in action as well as of old-fashioned service and fidelity.

On the way down in the lift, my mother was silent and there were tears in the corners of her eyes.

Sixty-Seven Small Faces

Rene Howden's small school at Sumach was such a success that when I was six she removed it to a much larger building with spacious gardens and mature trees, Lady Mede,* in the village of Little Kimble.

In front of me, I have the school photograph for 1949, and it contains sixty-seven children and four teachers. Sally, aged five, is sitting cross-legged in the front row, and with her generous forehead and somewhat epicanthic eyelids she looks very much her father's daughter. One summer day during this, her first year at Lady Mede, she came running round one side of the school to the croquet lawn. There a boy lay prostrate, with a great gash on his forehead, knocked cold by a wildly-swinging mallet.

Sally stared down and realised it was me.

'Arms outstretched, legs outstretched,' she says. 'White-faced and spreadeagled like a starfish. I thought you were dead.'

Although I have never really excelled in any sport, I have been proficient in several: a decent all-rounder with lots of

---

* The school is now called Ladymede.

enthusiasm but limited talent.

At Oxford, I played tennis, squash and hockey for my college but although I turned out from time to time for the Penguins – the university's second VI – I fell just short of playing representative tennis at that level on a regular basis.

Before this, at school, I'd also played cricket, football and rugby, and had a front tooth knocked out by a marauding forward. But at Lady Mede, my passion was for athletics, and my favourite day of the year was Sports Day.

In my last year, when I was nine and head boy, I was so confident of the Flat Race, as it was called, that I eased off and picked out my mother in the crowd near the finishing-tape and waved to her.

My mother was appalled. She yelled at me, but I thought she was cheering me on. And then I was overtaken.

True, I won the senior sports cup inscribed 'Victor Ludorum' and the *Bucks Advertiser* ran a small piece under the heading, 'Kevin Took Cup From His Mother'. Quite why it was my mother who was presenting the prizes, I have no idea but, predictably, she later read me the riot act about never having won or lost a race or a match until it was finished.

Her disapproval, however, was offset by her pleasure in the way I had coached Sally in the long jump.

'When you run up,' I instructed her, 'pretend it's high jump. The higher you jump, the longer you'll jump.'

At Lady Mede, I enjoyed history and geography, and found mental arithmetic very easy, as I've always done. My reports comment regularly on my great eagerness and enthusiasm but also draw attention to my impetuosity and carelessness. My arithmetic teacher was especially harsh on me: '*Disgusting*. Can't you set down a multiplying sum? . . . Will you please sharpen your pencil . . . your figures are so bad you can't read them yourself.' There are several suggestions that for all my apparent confidence, I was actually rather uncertain of myself and worried too much.

My favourite class, though, was music, taught by Mrs

Thomas, an energetic and spirited Welshwoman.

When Mrs Thomas picked me to sing the first verse of the opening carol at the Christmas concert, I felt a surge of joy: because I liked audiences, because I knew my father would be pleased, and because it impressed Mrs Thomas's daughter, Karen.

On the great day, I woke with a sore throat but was not to be put off. The hall filled with parents and grandparents, I stepped forward, and Mrs Thomas played the opening verse of 'The Holly and the Ivy'. Then she played the opening chord again and nodded at me.

'The holly and . . .' Croak!

Everyone laughed. Of course the laughter was sympathetic, but that's not how it sounded.

'That's all right, Kevin,' Mrs Thomas said. 'Try again.'

I did try again, and again the fearsome fifth defeated me. Croak!

I retreated to the ranks, overheated and desperate.

One day when I was seven, I came in to school late and discovered that I had missed my first Latin class. Before I was allowed to join everyone else for break, I had to copy out the six words on the blackboard.

Amo. Amas. Amat. Amamus. Amatis. Amant.

It was one thing to succumb to the present tense of one amatory verb, quite another to deal in gerunds and future perfects and the like, and before long my parents decided that my Latin needed reinforcing – I say 'parents' but, in all likelihood, it was my indefatigable mother; she made all the running in such matters.

Twice each week, after school, I had an hour-long Latin class with the Reverend Denys Roberts, the priest at Monks Risborough. On a third day, I had a piano lesson with Mrs Carwithen; and on each day, there was dreaded piano practice. In addition to all this, time had to be found for other 'extras': dancing classes, riding lessons and, after a while, viola lessons.

Amo, amas . . .

The first girl to whom I proposed, my mother told me, was called Jennifer. I was two.

'Will you marry me?' I asked her. And then without waiting for an answer, 'Can you cook?'

But the first girl who excited me was Karen, daughter of the musical Mrs Thomas. We were playing hide-and-seek at a party in the darkened hall at Lady Mede, and through my splayed fingers I watched her hide. I ran over to the piano, and crawled under it on all fours. I sought and caught Karen, and there I kissed her.

These sixty-seven small faces and small bodies (see opposite): what are their stories? Some are renowned, some died young, almost all I no longer know. But here's the sandy-haired boy who became a priest and here are the two daughters of a world-famous scientist, here is the girl with whom I sustained an intense correspondence during her year at a 'finishing school' in Switzerland, here is the boy who died of AIDS and the girl who showed me her vagina in return for a whole week's pocket-money (ninepence, at the time!) . . . The resolute and irresolute, the smiling and solemn, stocky and lanky, attentive and bored, open-eyed and squinting into the sunlight, what are their stories and how much can one read of them in these sunlit cameos?

I haven't studied this photograph for almost sixty years and, doing so now, I find the images of the children with whom I grew up intensely moving.

'Childlike, I danced in a dream,' says Thomas Hardy. And Thomas Traherne: 'I knew not that there were sins or complaints or laws. I dream'd not of poverties, contentions or vices. All tears and quarrels were hidden from my eyes. I saw all in the peace of Eden.'

So the letter I received many years later from Rene Howden exploded inside my head and heart like a thunderbolt.

In assembling an anthology for children of riddles ancient and modern, I had ill-advisedly included a couple of the black riddles that regularly circulate in secondary schools and else-

Sixty-seven small faces: Lady Mede school photograph (1949)

where after disasters. One was about the Argentinian General Galtieri and the other about Earl Mountbatten.

'Children,' I noted, 'and riddle-makers are no respecters of reputations or, indeed, atrocities.'

This was not good enough for the *Daily Telegraph*. On its front page it questioned the propriety of reprinting the Mountbatten riddle (but not the Galtieri one!), while one MP asked a question in the Commons about what the ex-Prime Minister's publishing house thought it was doing publishing a text by inference disloyal to the Crown.

My words of qualification weren't good enough for Rene Howden either, if indeed she ever read them for herself.

'You may not know,' she wrote, 'how we have all followed your career with great pride. You have utterly disgraced yourself, and I only hope that no one finds out you attended Lady Mede . . .'

The 1948 Olympics

Strange! I could have sworn that the 1948 Olympics were held at the White City.

True, my mother played county tennis for Bedfordshire, but until my nephew Ben rowed in the Commonwealth Games, much the most notable sportsman in our family was my father's brother, Dick. Before leaving Jesus College, Cambridge, in 1938 to serve in the navy, he won an athletics blue and then ran the mile as fourth string in the combined Oxford and Cambridge team against Harvard and Yale.

He ran it very fast indeed, in four minutes and nineteen seconds, and he ran it faster than anyone else.

My grandmother Neenie told me she was so overcome with excitement that all the strength went out of her own legs, and she had to sit down.

This famous victory was indeed won at the White City . . . and my mind has done the rest.

In actuality, the 1948 Olympic Games took place in the old Wembley Stadium, and that is where, one August morning, my mother conducted her extremely enthusiastic seven-year-old son.

These were the first Games to be held since the infamous 1936 Games in Berlin, and Germany and Japan were not invited to them. What I remember is the thrill of being in the middle of a huge cheering crowd for the first time in my life; my mother's regret at not seeing Fanny Blankers-Koen, the thirty-year-old Dutch housewife who won four track medals; and an overwhelming excitement at watching the 100 metres final, which resulted in a photo-finish between two Americans, Barney Ewell and Harrison Dillard, who won the gold medal. This was the first time, incidentally, in which starting-blocks had been used in the sprint races.

I'm a very competitive creature, and this natural instinct was fostered by my mother's own love of playing sport and by her unremitting efforts to take me as a boy to national sporting events.

I'm glad of this glitch in my memory, this dovetailing of events that for years has made my Uncle Dick's achievements of one breath with those of Blankers-Koen, Dillard and the incomparable Emil Zatopek, a rat-a-tat-tat of a name that calls out for rapid enunciation!

Now and then, someone asks me whether I'm related to my modest, handsome, bright blue-eyed uncle, who returned to Cambridge to complete his degree after the war, and I always feel pleased and proud.

The Then and Now of It

'Just put in it your pocket. Rumer will know how to tie it.'

I can hear my mother saying this, I can even see us both standing at the foot of the staircase beside the telephone, but it seems so completely unlike her: not knowing how to tie a single-ended bow tie, and willingly allowing as much to another woman.

So I walked out of Crosskeys into the frosty dark, wearing my hired dinner jacket, with a bow tie in my pocket. I was twelve.

In the quiet little village street, which is also the Upper Icknield Way, I knocked on the famous author's door and she admitted me to the small dinner-dance she was holding for her daughter Paula, a year older than me. In this way, Rumer Godden tied my first bow tie for me!

Rumer's cottage, Pollards, was so full of fragile wonders – especially glass and musical boxes – that I'm surprised she agreed to have a party at home for her daughter. She gave the impression of keeping raw life at arm's length, and regarded children as akin to bulls in a china shop.

Opposite Rumer's cottage was the village library. This was a small, creaky, wooden barn, and it opened just once a week for two hours, on Sunday afternoons.

The librarian was Miss Hill and her partner was Miss Nash – Barbara Nash – whom I now know to have been the sister of the painters John and Paul Nash. Together, they ran the local nursery garden, and I couldn't imagine how Miss Hill could bear to come indoors and spend even one hour in such cramped, gloomy and airless surroundings.

When I think about what I read and mainly did not read during the first twelve years of my life, I am perplexed and pained.

I got off to a quick start, and was able to say my alphabet at the age of two and a quarter, and as I have described my father delighted in singing-and-saying bedtime stories to Sally and me. After I'd graduated to my own room at the top of the stairs, I came down to the nursery before Sally's lights were turned off so the three of us could share them.

But although his study was walled with books (he was already winning a considerable reputation as a musicologist), my father only read for pleasure when on holiday in Norfolk each year. His diet was always the same: crime novels by Agatha Christie in their green-and-white Penguin Editions.

And writing this, I realise with some shock that my mother almost never read for pure pleasure. She read a certain amount for self-understanding, while with Sally and me she now and then shared a poem or a scene she already knew and loved, sometimes melancholy, usually humorous: a poem from Walter de la Mare's anthology *Peacock Pie* (I especially liked 'Linden Lea'), an episode from *Three Men in a Boat*, a chapter from *1066 and All That*.

My mother organised Sally's and my packed days from dawn to dusk, but neither she nor my father really encouraged us to read, except for a few minutes before lights out. From time to time they did buy me a new book, but the single row in my upstairs bedroom largely consisted of rather dismal-looking dusty volumes owned by my mother as a girl, and passed on to me.

Once, in the Indian hill-station of Kodaikanal in the Western Ghats, I came across a small glass-fronted case stuffed with books. Eagerly I opened it, thinking I might have stumbled on great wonders. What it contained were dowdy copies of children's books from the first two or three decades of the last century. My shelf was rather like that.

Here is *The Swiss Family Robinson*, inscribed by my mother in a girlish hand, and then by me. This edition of 'An account of a Swiss pastor and his family on an uninhabited island', as the racy subtitle tells us, was printed in 1920, and there are more than 400 words on each page. I can hear my mother saying, 'I can't understand why you can't get on with it. I loved it!'

Here are *The Water-Babies* and the foxed pages of the *Just So Stories* and *Treasure Island*. On the bleak endpaper I have written KEVIN C-H J W in a bold, disorderly hand, and facing the half-title, my grandmother has written in purple pencil: 'May 1948. To Kevin with fond love from Neenie to read when he is older'.

Neenie had absolutely no truck with any episode in a book that frightened me. She simply snip-snapped her scissors and cut it out!

It is not much use pretending to children that there are no horrors in the world, when they know perfectly well that there are. They know it daily from television and radio; they know it on the internet and from newspapers; they know it from loose talk among adults. There's a little story I've long been partial to that goes something like this:

> There was a young boy whose parents wanted to keep him safe from every kind of superstition, let alone naked atrocity. They never mentioned witches or giants or fiends. They never told him fairy tales. One night, the boy's parents were toasting their toes in front of the fire when they thought they heard – yes, they did! – a terrible

sobbing upstairs. They ran up to their son's room, and there he was, crying his eyes out. 'What's wrong?' they asked. 'What is it?' When he'd caught his breath, he told them he was afraid of sleeping in the dark. 'Why?' they asked. 'Why?' The boy began to sob again. 'Mummy . . .' Sob. 'Daddy . . .' Sob. 'There's a complex hiding under my bed.'

My parents' and Neenie's intentions were good – of course they were – but although I always pounced on my comic *Eagle* as soon as it dropped through the letterbox, they fostered in me no great love of reading. This said, there were a few exceptions, certainly: André Maurois's *Fattypuffs and Thinifers* (almost as good a title as the original *Patapoufs et Filifers*); a biography of Robert Schumann, taking desperate measures to save his little finger and ability to play the piano, going mad, throwing himself off a bridge – I've often thought since of writing for children about the lives of composers; *The Snow House* by Marian Johnston, *The Story of Shy the Platypus* by Leslie Rees, *The Story of a Red-Deer* by the Hon. J. W. Fortescue and *Out of Doors with Nomad: Further Adventures Among the Wild Life of the Countryside* by Norman Ellison (who was Nomad the Naturalist on BBC *Children's Hour*), superbly illustrated with C. F. Tunnicliffe's woodcuts; and, more predictably, *Winnie the Pooh* and *A Christmas Carol* and *The Wind in the Willows* and *Alice in Wonderland*. The endpapers of *Alice* are decorated with a sepia crocodile of characters, and beside the words *The Owner of this Book is* . . . I have inscribed 'Kevin crosle holend'. Seldom backward in coming forward, I have also pencilled my name beside Mabel Lucie Atwell's picture of Alice on the front boards of the book.

The only category of book that regularly interested me was historical fiction and, remembering the books on my shelf, it's plain that my parents did attempt to build on this. Here are spotted, fustian copies of *The Count of the Saxon Shore* by the Rev. Alfred J. Church, MA, published in 1887, and Charles

Kingsley's *Hereward the Wake*; Captain Marryat, Henty, Anthony Hope and my favourite, Baroness Orczy's *The Scarlet Pimpernel*:

> They seek him here, they seek him there,
> Those Frenchies seek him everywhere.
> Is he in heaven, is he in hell?
> That damned elusive Pimpernel.

But here, also, are a few books in dustcovers, brand-new when they were given to me: *Redcap Runs Away* by Rhoda Power, early Rosemary Sutcliff, and *The Wool-Pack* by Cynthia Harnett, winner of the Carnegie Medal.

There was one book on the shelf to which I returned dozens and dozens and perhaps even hundreds of times. This was *Our Island Story* by H. E. [Henrietta Elizabeth] Marshall, first published in 1905, recently reissued in a centenary edition.

This Edwardian classic retells scenes from British history in chronological order with great vividness and verve, and it thrilled me. I identified as never before with the hopes and fears and quests and achievements of Boudicca, Alfred, Harold Godwinson. I stared so long at A. S. Forrest's coloured pictures that I became the little boy stammering out my story to Henry I and the page witnessing the signing of the Great Charter, I was Flora Macdonald's ardent lover, and the noble who plucked a red rose and put it in my cap, and the boy with a rosebud mouth, one of that band of exiles who 'moor'd their bark on the wild New England shore'.

I have come to believe that it is through story, inviting identification and exciting the imagination, that children can most fruitfully develop a sense of history. I believe that each old coin and sherd contains its own story, if only you ask it who and what and where and how and why and when; if only you will dream. And I believe it is crucial that historical fiction should be well researched and well-written, eschewing archaism. Indeed, I've always subscribed to my old friend Jill Paton Walsh's elegant dictum that the historical novelist may admit the not known to be true but must reject the known not to be true.

Our Island Story is the cornerstone for this credo. And I suppose that my passion for encouraging and stimulating children to read may be all the greater because my parents did not succeed in getting me to do so.

From time to time, Sally and I sat and listened with my father to records (78s, of course) on the gramophone. At Crosskeys, the house rule for listening to music of any kind was that we should do so attentively and in silence, and never, never as background noise. This is a practice I have observed to this day. When my father was away, and we were making too much of a rumpus in our little cottage, my mother's solution was not to send us to our rooms to read but to make us sit down and listen to music.

Once, Tchaikovsky's *Pathétique* was being played on the radio, and my mother said she'd give us threepence each – half my weekly pocket money – if we kept quiet, side by side on the sofa, until the end of the symphony.

At the end of the jubilant, overwhelmingly exciting third movement, we fairly exploded across the room, leaping and waving.

'Very good!' my mother congratulated us. 'Well done!'

Then the forlorn, stricken finale began . . . *Adagio lamentoso*, the work of a man only ten days before his death.

Amused at her own ignorance and with an innate sense of fair play, my mother gave us each a threepenny bit and told us to 'pipe down'.

I must have borrowed books from our little hillside library, the Gow Library, memory of which, however, has been completely eclipsed by my guilt over the one I borrowed and failed to return.

I kept this book for three weeks. I kept it for four. And since I didn't fancy paying over part of my precious pocket money as a fine, I hid it under my mattress . . .

I kept the book for a whole year, moving it from time to time so that my mother wouldn't discover it. I kept it for four years.

I kept it for forty.

During those years, I fell in love with books. I fell in love with everything about them: the way they're made, the way they look, the different typefaces, the colour and weight of the paper, the way they smell. Above all, I fell in love with words, images, stories, lives, issues.

I began to borrow books from other libraries, hundreds and hundreds (and I returned them!). I tried to catch up with the books I never read as a boy, and I'm still trying. I bought books. My first job was in the publishing house of Macmillan.

But of course that one unreturned book kept gnawing at my conscience. What was worse, I could no longer find it. And after a while, most strangely, I could see exactly how it looked, its faded blue cloth, the gold lettering on its spine, but I could no longer even remember what it was about or its name.

In my late forties, I hit on a simple plan, partly to expiate my guilt, partly in the name of winning publicity. I decided to offer Whiteleaf library one copy of each book I had written. That, I thought, would settle the score. Wouldn't it?

I piled my books on to the back seat of my car and, as I drove across England, I was still thinking as much like an eight- as a forty-eight-year-old. They won't insist on the fine, will they? Will they charge compound interest? What if they don't see the funny side of this? Surely they can't put me in prison for petty theft?

It was some years since I had returned to Whiteleaf. I gazed at Crosskeys, and the towering chalk cross; I read the graffiti in the wooden bus shelter; I strolled down the village street . . . the library was not there.

Opposite the cottage where Rumer Godden had lived, the library had simply vanished. The books, all the books, the wooden barn that housed them, Miss Hill: they had all disappeared. There was just a gap – a hole in my heart – where they had been.

'It fell down,' an old villager told me.

'Fell?'

'Years ago.'

'When?'

He chewed a piece of grass and considered me.

'Oh dear!' I said. I felt quite hopeless.

He sniffed and chewed the grass some more. 'It was only books!' he said. 'What's that to you?'

Not long ago, I went to see an old friend, the author Ronald Blythe, at Bottengom's, the hidden East Anglian long house once owned by his longstanding and dear friends, John and Christine Nash. We began to talk about Whiteleaf, and I told him about Miss Nash and Miss Hill.

First he led me over to look at Paul Nash's vibrant pencil drawing of his sister, Barbara. And then, before I left, Ronnie gave me an ineffable smile and a gift: a lovely lithograph, sepia and umber and black by Francis Sydney Unwin. Unwin had taught John Nash the technique of etching when they were briefly next-door neighbours in the village immediately after the war, before John and Christine Nash moved to Lane End in the nearby village of Meadle, where they lived for eighteen years.

And Unwin's lithograph? It depicted one wooden, rather tumbledown building, somehow hugging itself, an ancient keeper of secrets: the Gow Library at Whiteleaf.

Better Than All Books

An old house packed with memories . . .

   Not only did I remove offending elements of the landscape when I sat on the hilltop; charged with my father's stories and speculations, and by stirring episodes in *Our Island Story*, I restored those that had been ruined or lost in the dark drum-roll of years.

   I gave back to Saint Dunstan's, the church at Monks Risborough, nestling under the foot of the hill, its glorious multicoloured medieval self; I planted a great forest of oak and ash and elm and beech stretching out across the Vale of Aylesbury into Oxfordshire; once more the Iron Age ramparts on Cymbeline's Mount bustled and bristled:

> Eyes at the interstices,
> Regular, round as compasses and clocks;
> And behind ramparts, hidden from without,
> Orderly mounds of slingstones, small forests
> Of ash-spears, sunstruck shields and bodyguards,
> All the gear, ready.*

* *The Dream-House:* from 'Fortification'.

Above all, the Icknield Way quickened my imagination. Once, my parents took Sally and me to see Stonehenge and Silbury hill; and often, we drove away up to the North Norfolk coast and spent part of our holidays there with my grandparents. Sitting on Whiteleaf Cross, I stared down at this Neolithic trackway, or at least the hedgerows flanking it, linking North Norfolk and Wiltshire, and I imagined it peopled with traders carrying heavy, uncomfortable nubs of flint, tin, leather, walrus tusks, amber and cornelian . . .

The stretch that runs south-west from Whiteleaf has scarcely changed since it was walked by Edward Thomas:

> I climbed up past 'The Red Lion' at Whiteleaf . . . and went down a hedged and rutty lane, leaving the spire of Princes Risborough half a mile below on the right. The way was some distance up on a steep slope, and itself in places so steep from side to side that there were two tracks, one two yards above the other. Then it was a broad track of level turf . . . the ruts, as near the Horsenden road, mended with lemonade bottles and meat tins. *

The Romans adopted part of the Icknield Way and, after it had rained for days and the track was soft and muddy, I sometimes used to walk down it, prodding it with my little Swiss walking stick in the hope of striking Roman paving-stones. In this I was disappointed, but it was easy to imagine legionaries marching through my village, just as Thomas Hardy imagined them in Dorset:

> The Roman Road runs straight and bare
> As the pale parting-line in hair
> Across the heath. And thoughtful men
> Contrast its days of Now and Then,
> And delve, and measure and compare;

* Edward Thomas: *The Icknield Way* (1913).

70

Visioning on the vacant air
Helmed legionaries, who proudly wear
The Eagle . . . *

I was so eager to find signs and scraps of evidence of earlier generations. With my father, I patiently trudged for hours along the furrows of freshly ploughed fields on Bledlow Ridge, and came home caked in mud, pockets stuffed with potsherds – and these I used to wash and lay out in their hundreds like pieces of jigsaw, and vainly try to fit together. I braved the tilting and topsy gravestones in Monks Risborough churchyard to check out new crops of molehills until, one summer evening when I was nine, two friends from Lady Mede lay in wait for me there, and rose up from behind gravestones, each wearing a white sheet and moaning.

That same summer, my parents took Sally and me on a long round-the-Chilterns drive, stopping to look at sundry places that had associations for them. When we came to the extremely steep escarpment of Ivinghoe Beacon, my father told me how, as a boy, he had started to run down it and then been unable to stop. And by the time he got to the bottom, he said, 'I was running so fast that I jumped right over the road.'

I didn't disbelieve him, but I was less impressed by my father's prodigious leap, only possible for a magician, than concerned with what would have happened if 'a car had been coming'.

'What if a car had been coming?' I can still hear myself saying it, sitting in the back of BTM812. 'What if a car had been coming?'

Not at all the response my father had hoped to elicit.

Below the Beacon, and near now to the end of the day, we stopped at the head of a precipitous valley, almost a chasm, known as Coombe Hole and Coombe Bottom.

'This is where Boadicea,' my father told me, using the old pronunciation, 'fought her last battle against the Romans.'

That was it! Despite my parents' protests, I was out of the

* 'The Roman Road'.

car and helter-skeltering down the scree on to the grassy slope below. I searched; I stared down the valley at the Roman army marching up towards me, trapping Boadicea and her blue Iceni henchmen at the head of the valley; I searched again; I could hear my mother and father calling for me.

'Nothing,' I reported when I had scrambled back up to the car.

'What do you mean?'

Over the years, my mother often reminded me of my deflated reply. 'Well, I thought I'd at least find a bottle of woad, or something.'

Or something!

My father and I went walking and, as usual, each of us had one eye on the bright world around us, one eye on the ground.

I suppose we must have been talking about what we'd unearthed on our last walk, or some such, because my father said, 'Today, let's find a Roman coin.'

We walked south from Whiteleaf to Kop Hill,* overlooking Princes Risborough and a surviving portion of the burgeoning Black Hedge, more than one thousand years old. We stared at patches of rough ground where the grass had withered and the soil was exposed; as usual, we kicked over molehills. Nothing, not even a sherd or a flint that might have been knapped. On the brow of the hill, there were a number of small, scrubby bushes.

'Just have a look under them,' my father told me.

On all fours, I scrambled under a couple of bushes, and inspected the soft, shadowed topsoil. Nothing and nothing. Under the third bush was a little dark disk I took to be the top of a spent cartridge case – there were plenty of those on the hills and in the high woods.

I picked it up. It was the size of a five-pence piece, delicate, thinner than an ice-cream wafer, slightly ragged round the edge.

* Ordnance Survey has it both ways, calling the main hill Kop but the knoll immediately south of it Risborough Cop. The hill acquired its 'K' after the Boer War.

'What have you got?' my father asked me. His voice came from miles away.

Looking out of the coin was a small, wreathed head.

I backed out and stood up. I turned over the little disk and my father and I stared at it without a word.

There, on the flat of my grubby palm, were two soldiers, each holding a spear. And round the rim letters, words chased one another . . .

I don't remember what my father or I said, only my over-whelming sense of excitement at making such a find, such a direct link to the life of another person, the boy or girl or grown-up who had dropped or hidden this coin, here on this hill.

It wasn't long before I was looking at the coin through a magnifying-glass, and my father helped me to establish that it was a Constantine, a copper denarius portraying the Emperor who had ruled from AD 272 to 337 and was converted to Christianity.

Thomas Hardy again! In 'In the Old Theatre, Fiesole', he describes how, in the hills overlooking Florence, a girl showed him a Constantine, raising his awareness of the legacy of Rome 'better than all books':

> For in my distant plot of English loam
> 'Twas but to delve, and straightway there to find
> Coins of like impress. As with one half blind
> Whom common simples cure, her act flashed home
> In that mute moment to my opened mind
> The power, the pride, the reach of perished Rome.

To begin with, I did wonder whether my father had planted my Constantine under that bush on Kop Hill, in the same sort of way that a child suspects he or she is being allowed to win some game. But he would never have done anything quite as crude as that and, anyhow, I was ignoring his great gift of serendipity.

In the event, my sneaking suspicion was soon proved to be

completely unfounded.

In Princes Risborough High Street, there was a chemist, Padley's, to whom Sally and I sold rose-hips for fourpence per pound – a small, seasonal supplement to our meagre pocket money. A few months after I found my Constantine, the shop had an unusual item for sale alongside the unlabelled bottles of rose-hip syrup: a little nest of twenty-eight Roman coins, found together on Kop Hill.

They cost five shillings and, with some help from my parents and a great deal of self-sacrifice, my sister Sally bought them all for me as a Christmas present.

Twenty-eight Roman coins. Twenty-nine, including my own! Who hid them there? And why were they never reclaimed? How I treasured this little hoard. It was my pride and joy.

Bicycling

Both my parents well understood the power of ritual, and for my father Christmas was pure theatre.

When we were young children, Sally and I were not allowed to see the Christmas tree, erected in my father's study behind closed curtains, until after tea on Christmas Day. We had to wait outside the door while he lit all the candles on the tree (an appalling fire risk) and my mother tried to straighten them. As soon as he had called us in, he cut off a small branch and held it to the fire. It crackled and smoked. Then he loped round, waving it until the whole room became fuzzy with sweet, acrid smoke, and our eyes were smarting.

Early on Christmas morning, Sally and I brought our stockings to our parents' bedroom, and clambered into bed between them. My mother was bright-eyed, my father frustratingly dopey.

Then, after breakfast and before church, we opened some but not all of our main presents. My father kept a list of gifts and donors, and I wasn't supposed to play with a present until I had written a thank-you letter for it.

I had longed so much for a bike that maybe my longing half-blinded me. I stared at the presents under the tree, but they were all far too small. I stared and stared and I remember the hot tears behind my eyes.

'Well!' said my mother. 'Haven't you seen it?'

It was half-hidden behind the tree, leaning against the wall: a bicycle, second-hand, repainted by my father postbox red.

To begin with, I was allowed to ride around the village, but not outside it. Proudly, I took it to show my friend James, but he had been given an airgun for Christmas and invited me to have a go with it. With trepidation, I loaded it with a lead pellet and from his bedroom window shot at a red squirrel sitting up in a tree in the middle of the lawn. I missed, the squirrel scampered away, but I've felt guilty about this ever since.

My bike had a small basket strapped to the handlebars, and on a second visit I put my unwanted presents into it and swapped them with James's. Our parents were distinctly unimpressed, and made us both give them back.

Then Ian Agnew came cycling from Great Kimble to see me, and he had been given a bike too – a new one. But when, six weeks later, my parents presented me with a speedometer for my birthday, my joy was complete.

As soon as it had been fixed, I rode along the narrow village street, and picked up speed as the road dipped down past The Red Lion . . .

At the tight corner there, I fell off, and the driver of the pale green car coming towards me jammed on his brakes.

'It's a good thing it was the doctor,' I told my mother later, as she put stinging TCP and plasters on my elbows and ankles and knees.

'Why?'

'He might have run over me otherwise.'

On the whole, it's remarkable I didn't have more accidents. I used to wheel my bike up the lane above our cottage, round a hair-raising corner I long believed to be one-in-three, as one used to say, but was probably one-in-four or one-in-five, until I reached the point where the tarmac was always white because of the regular chalkfall from the Cross. From there, I rode pell-mell down the hill, past our cottage, past the village street, and hurtled down steep Peter's Lane to the main Aylesbury–Wycombe road at the bottom.

Several times, scarcely daring to look but looking at my speedometer, I reached 40 mph – the top speed on the dial. I wondered what would happen if I went even faster than that. Would the speedometer break? And what if one of the bumps in the road threw me off balance, or a farm machine came out of the hole in the hedge near the bottom, or my brakes failed? But none of this stopped me.

When Sally was given a bike, I used to run round and round our little lawn, holding the back of her seat, egging her on. And as soon as she could ride with some confidence, our parents allowed us out together.

How they trusted us, always giving us as much latitude as they could, yet never for one moment letting go of the reins. And how they trusted in our neighbourhood. I remember only one occasion when my mother told us she wanted us to stay at home and play in the garden.

'Why?' I demanded.

'There's a murderer in the woods,' she replied. And that was the end of the matter.

By the time I was eleven and Sally was eight, we were allowed to ride much further afield with the proviso that our parents knew where we were going. We were sometimes away for most of the day.

We pedalled past the Sanatorium at Saunderton, best known for its treatment of TB, and rode eight miles along the main road to West Wycombe, where I stared up at the mausoleum and the golden ball above the church of Saint Lawrence. Made of gilded fabric stretched over a wooden frame, there's seating for twelve people inside it, and my imagination turned flame-red as I visualised the meetings there of Sir Francis Dashwood's Hell Fire Club and talk of devil worship or, anyhow, drunken revelries. On the way back, I got a multiple puncture, if there is such a thing, and being unable to mend it, trudged a mile to the nearest telephone box to ring my mother, and ask her to come and collect us.

Strapped for cash as usual, Sally and I started to make and paint small ceramic bowls and ramekins and tried to sell them. I was so eager to get quick results that I didn't bother to paint the undersides. When the owner of a craft shop in Aylesbury was generous and unwise enough to buy one, Sally and I really applied ourselves and soon set off for town again, our wickerwork bicycle baskets laden with many more.

One summer morning, I decided to ride over to see my treasure-hunt partner, raven-haired Ann, and I suppose it's because of my growing feelings for her that I remember this pilgrimage so well, almost each wheel-turn of it. The voltage of an early experience plainly sharpens one's memory of it.

My mother made me a picnic and, after cycling past the third green of Whiteleaf golf course and down to Askett, where I had gone to Sumach school, I struck out for enchanting Meadle where, as so often, I paused for refreshment outside Lane End, the house that had once belonged (not that I knew it) to John and Christine Nash. Then I headed for the deserted medieval village at Waldridge, and then for Ford and Dinton, deep in the Vale of Aylesbury.

It was so hot that there were globs of glistening tar on the road. I sat against a barred fence, and sucked at the cheddar cheese stuck between my teeth, and sluiced it down with the tepid elderflower cordial made by my father. The piece of chocolate my mother had put in for me was as soft and shiny as the tar.

Then I got out my jack-knife. For most of the time now it rests in one of my peaceful desk drawers, but now and then I rediscover it, and whittle a piece of wood with it, as I used to do.

The lane was so quiet that not one car had passed while I was eating my picnic. Hurriedly, I began to hack at one of the cat's eyes in the middle of the road. The rubber pad was much tougher and thicker than I had expected; but jabbing and sawing, I managed to 'liberate' one, and pocketed it.

Cat's eyes are a simple, brilliant device and made Percy Shaw, their inventor, rich. But after seventy-five years it seems they have more or less had their day. Several times recently, while driving along Norfolk lanes, the ones that recall lost innocence, I have seen the sign CATS EYES HAVE BEEN REMOVED. Each time, it makes me jump.

When I had crossed the main road from Aylesbury to Oxford, I went to inspect the strange folly in Dinton, built in 1749 by Sir John Vanhattem who stored his collection of fossils, including vast ammonites, in the limestone walls. Then I pedalled into Cuddington, where Ann's mother, tall and elegant, led me into the cool drawing-room of the Old Rectory.

'Ann's up in the loft,' she said. 'I expect you'd like to wash first, would you?'

I climbed the ladder and there she was, sitting cross-legged, wearing a band in her hair and a simple blue-and-white crosshatched dress. There she was, with a lapful of windfalls.

The loft smelt sweet and sour, like the attic at Crosskeys; my throat was dry.

Certain childhood moments, certain images impress themselves indelibly on our minds; even to think of them may bring us close to tears.

That loft, and Ann sitting there, and those apples, like temptations, like feelings, like words . . .

'Oh good!' said Ann. 'Can you help me sort these out?'

I can't pretend to remember whether I dawdled or pedalled furiously on the way home. Both, most likely.

Not far west of Askett, there was and still is a small hump bridge over the railway line. Just short of it, I fell off my bike, face first, into a bed of stinging nettles.

My face and arms and legs were scalded; my eyes ran.

At first, there was nothing but pain. Then I found dock leaves growing right next to the dusty nettles, as they so often do, and their green hands soothed me.

As if from nowhere, a little early evening wind got up from somewhere, and it cooled me.

I stared at Whiteleaf Cross, two miles away but already rising over me, shimmering and beckoning.

Burnham Overy Staithe

Sally and I scrambled into the back of the Morris Ten, and we were off.

Our early excitement lasted about as far as Halton Camp, maybe Dunstable Downs, but was soon snuffed out by the actuality of the long wearisome journey following the chalk seam north and east away from the Chilterns into East Anglia.

The gliders high above the Downs in their own dreamworld; the twenty-four-mile-stretch between Royston and Newmarket that somehow seemed like a no-man's-land; the little restaurant on the outskirts of Newmarket where often we stopped for lunch, and where I always chose cherry pie and ice-cream for dessert; the miles of high fencing around the American airbase at Lakenheath: there were dozens of landmarks such as these, dear because familiar.

Once, we stopped to picnic beside the perimeter fence, and then I needed to do 'a big one' and, while my trousers were around my ankles, a large bomber approached me, no more than one hundred feet high, about to land. I couldn't have been more alarmed if a wasp had flown between my bare buttocks. Absolutely convinced that it was aiming straight for me, I ran half-naked and yelling down the side of the road until the innocent bomber had passed overhead.

In Brandon, the Flintknappers Arms invariably led on to conversation designed to quell Sally and me, and stop active warfare breaking out in our poorly sprung, dark-blue leather back seat: talk about the practice of knapping; talk about my father's set of Boer War gunflints, and about the Neolithic flint mines just a few miles ahead at Grime's Graves, a name I always thought extremely sinister and a place I associated with all kinds of atrocities. I may not have been far wrong. 'Grime's' probably derives from Grim, one of the many names for Odin, the terrifying god of inspiration and war. Indeed, I still find Thetford Forest intimidating and drive through it as rapidly as I can.

After this, we were on the last leg of our journey, and I urged my father to drive faster. With the early ambition of being a sports commentator, I sat behind his shoulder, talking nonstop: 'Now Stirling Holland is putting his foot on it, there's a long straight here, two miles, pine trees on the right, a bend at the top. Stirling Holland can overtake . . . he can overtake . . . he can take the lead!'

On and on; on and on. It must have exasperated him but, mild as ever, all my father said from time to time was 'Pipe down, Kevin!' and, in extremis, 'Kevin! WILL you pipe down!'

The last part of our annual summer journey to North Norfolk was accompanied by mantras and rituals. As we drove through Swaffham, my father, Sally and I chanted, 'Swaffham, Swaffham, good for nawthen', and, approaching Fakenham, 'Fakenham, where they're maken'em, Fakenham, where they're maken'em.' Unable to sing in tune, my mother remained silent.

Leaving Fakenham, Sally and I began to sing a simple third over and over again, a pair of semi-quavers and a pair of quavers: 'Burn-ham Mar-ket, Burn-ham Mar-ket, Burn-ham Mar-ket . . .'

Before entering Burnham Overy, and just when we thought he had forgotten, my father wound down his window to admit the salt air, and announced, 'A penny for the first to see the windmill.'

In February 1929, my grandparents had bought four little fishermen's cottages in Burnham Overy Staithe, two in East Harbour Way to let, and two opposite the Moorings Hotel (owned and run by the Phillips family) to convert into their own holiday home. This my grandfather called Rahere after the physician who founded Saint Bartholomew's Hospital.

To my eyes, Rahere was full of wonders, and I inspected them all with great satisfaction as well as noting, with a child's ruthless eye, where there had been any changes since our previous visit.

In the kitchen, I energetically pumped up water from the well, and loved the way it spurted into the sink and splashed all over the draining-board and the floor; in the sitting room I opened the little cupboard fronted with the spines of old books, and verified that my grandfather still used purple ink; in the dining room, I stared at the carved figure of my ancestress, Joan Holland, the Fair Maid of Kent; I clambered up the extremely steep staircase and, in the landing cupboard, checked the stock of Kilner jars full of gooseberries, raspberries, samphire, shallots and the like, preserved and pickled by my grandmother during the preceding year.

But before all this! The moment we arrived, my grandfather would say, 'Now drop everything! Sit down! Joan, what will you drink?'

Sit down! This was the last thing Sally and I wanted to do. We wanted to rush up to our room, out of the house, down to the creek, away . . . But for the first few minutes, we had to sit politely with our orange or lemon barley water while my parents and Grandpa Frank sipped gin-and-tonic and Neenie had her usual – this was 'Coffin Varnish', an excruciating mixture of sweet sherry and gin.

But then we were 'excused' for just a few minutes and, fair weather or foul, we crossed the coast road and sprinted down to the little staithe, no more than two hundred yards away.

At our backs was the boatyard, with a special small field reserved then as now for Sharpies, and the black face and blind eyes of the Maltings.

In front of us was the tidal creek, maybe fifty yards across, flowing or on the drag, sometimes yapping, sometimes lost in a long sliding dream, and beyond the creek stretched the wilderness of the saltmarshes with their byzantine network of little creeks and channels and drains, their unblinking pulks or marsh pools.

And beyond the marshes! Beyond the marshes lay the glorious tidal island of Scolt Head. When I was twenty-three, this is how I celebrated it:

There it was, the island.

Low-slung sandhills like land-waves, fettered by marram.
One hut, a dark nugget. Across the creeks gleaming like
tin, like obsidian, across the marshes almost rust,
olive, serge, fawn, purpled for a season, the island.

We shoaled on the Staithe, stared out and possessed it;
children who collar half the world with a shout, and
share it in a secret.

Old men sat on a form lodged against the wall.
Of course we did not ask. We knew. They were too old.

There it was, and at times not there. Atmosphere
thickened, earth and air and water became one lung;
we were in a wilderness.

In a coat of changing colours it awaited us. In the
calm seas of our sleep it always loomed, always ahead.
We woke, instantly awake. As if we never had been
tired, and all things were possible.

So the boat came for us. The island stretched out to
us and we took it for granted. And no one asked by
which creeks we had come or could return.*

There was a ladder propped against the wall of the Maltings. At the top was a black door and inside the door, in a single, fascinating, pungent, salty room, lived Sheila Disney.

* *Selected Poems*: 'The First Island'.

Miss Disney made me nervous. A knobble-kneed, no-nonsense schoolteacher at Culford who later retired to Burnham Overy Staithe, she taught children to swim in Dead Man's Pool (also known as Bank Hole) and, going down on one knee, fired the rifle to start the annual Marsh Race. She dismissed my suggestion that she might be distantly related to Walt Disney but told me that one of her ancestors might have been a seal-woman. Having heard Shetlandic and Orcadian stories of seal-folk from my father, I had no reason to disbelieve this.

Sheila Disney used to catch her breakfast with her feet. She began each day with a swim and then waded down the creek until, prehensile as she was, she trapped a dab or flounder under her toes. In my imagination, she became over the years a kind of wildwoman embodying the fascination and danger of the creeks and saltmarshes:

> Easterlies have sandpapered her larynx.
> Webbed fingers, webbed feet:
> last child of a seal family.
>
> There is a blue flame at her hearth, blue
> mussels at her board.
> Her bath is the gannet's bath.
>
> Rents one windy room at the top of a ladder.
> Reeks of kelp.
>
> 'Suffer the little children,' she barks
> and the children – all the little ones –
> are enchanted.
>
> She has stroked through the indigo of
> Dead Man's Pool
> and returned with secrets.
>
> They slip their moorings. They
> tack towards her glittering eyes.*

* *Selected Poems*: from 'Waterslain: Diz'.

'I spy strangers,' barked a gruff voice behind us, and above us.

Sally and I whirled round and there was Miss Disney, standing at the top of the ladder.

'Are you coming up?'

'We've only just got here.'

'Tomorrow, then.'

That first evening, Sally and I shook the long journey out of our limbs, but we still felt like strangers. But when, very early the next morning, as cool air flowed through our little leaded window with amber and burgundy diamonds of glass let into it, and our black wooden floorboards creaked without our even standing on them, it dawned on us where we were, and we joyfully reclaimed Rahere and Norfolk as our own.

Ahead of us lay the bright day, and with luck our first picnic on 'the island'. But of course everything always took too long! By the time we finally set off, Sally and I had already run rings round Neenie's garden, lovingly stocked with rose and lavender bushes, and played hopscotch on the faded coloured tiles in the courtyard, and gone to see Mrs Riches in the post office, who invariably gave each of us a screw of peardrops in a conical white paper bag to get our holidays off to a good start.

Neenie didn't often come out with us, though she would have liked to do so. She felt obliged to stay behind, and prepare breakfast-in-bed for my grandfather, who never appeared before noon but sat up in bed, flanked by books and newspapers.

'I need time to prepare the evening meal, boy,' she said, 'and do bits and pieces around the house.'

These bits and pieces increased from day to day while we were staying at Rahere. Sally and I brought back samphire, sticky with marsh mud, and it needed to be washed several times before it was edible; we brought back shells and stones, seacoal and witches' purses and salt-eaten spars of wood, and scattered them around the courtyard; despite washing our feet in bowls of warm water laid before us in the courtyard as soon as we came in, we shed sandgrains up the staircase and across

1 With my parents and Sally on a Crossley Comfort, Bruce at our feet (1949)

2 My maternal grandparents, Claude and Mary Cowper, on their wedding day (1906)
3 Irene, Clive and Claude Cowper, flanked by my father and Sally, and me on an elephant

4 Crosskeys in summer
5 Grandpa Frank (1911)
6 Neenie (1911)

7 Whiteleaf Hill and Cross by Andy Rafferty
8 View from the top of Whiteleaf Cross by Alison Doggett

9 My mother and father on their wedding day
10 My mother, potting (1937)
11 My father, playing the Welsh harp (1949)

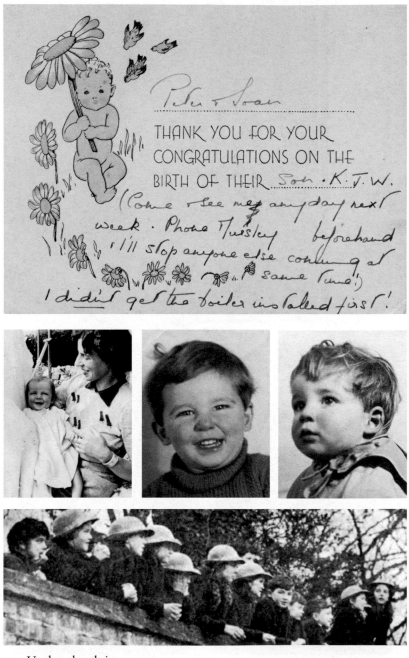

Peter & Joan

THANK YOU FOR YOUR CONGRATULATIONS ON THE BIRTH OF THEIR Son · K.J.W.

(Come & see me any day next week. Phone Twisley beforehand & I'll stop anyone else coming at same time!) I didn't get the boiler installed first!

12 Under the daisy . . .
13 Isn't he awful!
14 Turtle-necked
15 Ready for rain
16 At Lady Mede: an eye to the main chance (fifth from right)

17 From a contact sheet, aged three
18 With Bruce – and with tie. Aged eight

19 With Neenie in Wengen
20 The Belvedere Hotel, Wengen and the Jungfrau

the landing; we brought back pails of scooting shrimps.

Returning one morning from some outing, I was disappointed that Neenie had not already boiled the previous day's catch, as instructed.

'I haven't had time, boy,' Neenie said.

'They're getting impatient!' I told her.

Not that I would ever have dreamed of eating a single shrimp myself. But my mother and father sometimes obligingly had them on toast for breakfast while I watched them intently, and checked they ate each and every last one.

Sometimes we slogged out across the sands to the island; sometimes we walked past the ribs of Old Stoker's boat and along the cockle path, crossing precarious little bridges over channels with steep muddy sides, plunging one foot up to the knee, up to the hip, in a mud-hole; and sometimes, when the tide was right, we took a ride with Billy Haines on the *Rosemary*, the clinker-built boat he used as a ferry between Overy Staithe and Scolt Head and had motored right round to the south coast to take part in the relief of Dunkirk.

'C'm on, then, me bootie!' exhorted Billy, always in waders, as he handed us up the gangplank. I thought he had brighter blue eyes than anyone in the world except for my uncle Dick.

'That's because they've both spent so much time at sea,' my mother told me. 'The light got into them.'

Out on the island, we always made a bee-line for our own pocket in the dunes, and Sally and I were very put out on the rare occasions we already found it occupied.

There we spread out our towels, and got sand in our sandwiches – why else should they be so named? – and, fringed by spiky marram, inhabited our own small, often baking, incomparable kingdom.

Lying there, we could see nothing but sky. But the moment we stood up, we had unbroken views to south and west over a great complex of saltmarshes, shingle ridges, sand dunes and shining creeks. To our north and east lay the sea.

I would very much like to think that in this wild and beautiful place with their two young children, my parents were tolerably happy, despite the limitations of their marriage. Perhaps at times they were. But my mother found Grandpa Frank overbearing and pompous, though undeniably interesting, while she and Neenie were more mutually respectful and fond than loving or compatible (my mother so independent and quick-witted, Neenie so submissive and with relatively limited horizons), and in my grandmother's eyes her sons could do no wrong.

During our summer visits to Norfolk, moreover, my parents were exposed to each other's company for two unbroken weeks, and part of the reason for my mother's distaste for Burnham Overy Staithe was the lonely time she had endured there after the shock of finding out my father was having an affair. It was there that she and my father had to address their marriage – my father was never good at addressing conflict in personal relationships – and to make painful decisions.

Time and old age did not soften my mother's view of the Burnhams. 'I never really enjoyed our holidays in Norfolk,' she told me. 'I've never really understood your passion for it.' And then, with a pinch of scorn that had me rushing to Neenie's defence, 'Your grandmother was a nice little woman.'

But if I close my eyes and open my eyes? I can see a boy and a girl and their parents, still in their mid-thirties, weaving their way along the strand. Wherever there is nothing but sand, they quicken their steps; but wherever there are strips or ridges of shingle, their pace slows, they bow their heads, now and then they bend down and pick something up.

These four questors are searching for pieces of cornelian, the semi-precious quartz that can be as pale as palest orange marmalade, or scarlet as drops of new blood.

Now and then, one of the children hurries over to their father and shows him the latest find.

He holds it up to the light.

'Well!' he says, gently smiling. 'Third Grade' or 'Fourth Grade'. Or even 'Second Grade'.

'But when it's wet . . .' the boy protests.

'Lick it, Daddy,' says the girl.

I don't remember whether my father ever accorded one of my pieces the accolade of 'First Grade'. Probably not. He always mixed praise with qualification, knowing I would hear it as an incentive to further endeavour.

So I have been searching all my life for pieces of cornelian, and the best of them make their way into the small family hoard now displayed on an oblong glass plate.

Each time I make my way along a Norfolk beach, I follow the shingle ridges, and search until all the pebbles seem virtually the same sepia and crunch my brains, still almost believing that today or tomorrow, I will at last find the perfect, waiting piece.

I have many pages of notes for an unwritten poem, 'The Cornelian-Gatherers', that revolves around any artist's lifelong quest for the inexpressible. Dear God, even Mozart sat at the piano and wept because he could not write down the notes he heard, or almost heard.

In the Back Seat

Although I had no love of libraries, books or reading, I decided to write a book. Why not? Three years before, when I was six, I'd written *I LOVE THE WATRIS* and it had impressed and won me a kiss from its dedicatee. At school, just before term ended I'd completed a project about Ritchie Calder and an attempt to cultivate the Sahara, as well as making a frieze, 'The Road of History', while at home I kept an enormous scrapbook begun for me by my great-aunt Katie in Montreal.

My subject seemed obvious. Fired by my reading of *Our Island Story* and the layers of the landscape around me, inspired by my new learning, I resolved to embark on a *History of the World*.

This modest undertaking was a godsend to my mother. Heavily involved in social survey work throughout the summer of 1950, she now needed only to find somewhere to park Sally since I was happy to ride with her and, while she conducted her lengthy interviews, sit in the back of the car and write.

And that, I realise, is what I still do! When there are too many interruptions in the house, I drive off to the creek or to a quiet by-road, solemnly decamp from the driver's seat into the back, and write!

On one occasion, my mother asked me to help her. We went to County Council offices – in Hemel Hempstead, I think. I remember being glad that it was a long way away from Whiteleaf, in another county, and that maybe no one would notice my mistake.

My mother and I were given a stack of sheets listing thousands and thousands of names and addresses in alphabetical order. An electoral roll, I suppose. Then my mother asked me to start counting until I got to the two hundred and seventy-third name.

'Copy out that name and the address,' she told me. 'Check you've got the address right.'

I counted and showed my mother my handiwork.

'Very good,' she said. 'Now do the same again!'

'What?'

'Count until you get to the next two hundred and seventy-third name . . .'

After I'd repeated this dismal procedure several times, I lost count. I couldn't remember whether I was just entering the one hundred and twenties or repeating them. I hesitated, made sure my mother hadn't noticed, and then pressed on.

'What would happen,' I asked my mother on the way home late that afternoon, 'if anyone lost count and wrote down the wrong name?'

Did I really believe she would fail to see through such a question? Perhaps I half-wanted to be found out and reassured, but my mother wasn't letting me off so easily.

I was sitting in the back of the car and my mother looked at me in the rearview mirror. 'When one number's wrong,' she said, keeping a straight face, 'all the numbers after it are wrong as well. Aren't they! So then I'd be interviewing all the wrong people.' Mercifully, she chose to leave it at that.

While my mother visited her interviewees, right or wrong, I set to work (I brought along *Our Island Story*, officially as something solid to 'press on', and from time to time I read it furtively, with a sense that I was cheating). Of course it wasn't at all long before I felt hopelessly out of my depth. At the end of the third week, I realised I knew very, very much less than I thought I did about world history, and that it would be sensible to write something altogether less ambitious.

I knew what: *History of the British Isles*.

As a boy, I always wanted quick results, a tendency I finally grew out of, and I think I managed some seventy pages, beginning with the arrival of the Romans in 54 BC, before running out of steam. I wrote about a 'wise but naughty prince called Vortigern', and I wrote about King Arthur, asleep under Whiteleaf Cross, and about Alfred, the only king we have ever called 'Great', popularly known in medieval times as '*Engle hyrde, Engle deorling*', the shepherd of the English, the darling of the English. I wrote about Edmund Ironside, whose name appealed to me greatly, and wrote feelingly about poor Harold Godwinson's dilemma, having to face in two directions at the same time, and fight against Harald Hardrada and the Vikings in the north and Duke William and the Normans in the south. I wrote disparagingly about the Conqueror and admiringly about Hereward, betrayed in the Fens by 'wicked monks', and in red ink I copied out Blondel's song as he searched for Coeur-de-Lion, who 'was shut up in a castle in Germany and completely icelated from anyone else'.

But my great oeuvre breaks off in 1387 without mentioning Joan Holland and her marriages to Sir Thomas Holland and the Black Prince. Alas, I never got as far as Agincourt and the part one of my forebears may have played in it, let alone the life of Horatio Nelson, born in North Norfolk at Burnham Thorpe, only three miles away from my grandparents' cottage, or the accession in 1837 of young Queen Victoria, whom I knew to have loved nearby Sandringham House, and to have had singing lessons with Prince Albert there from Felix Mendelssohn.

So the summer holidays quickened and passed, and a new

school awaited me.

They had begun, as did each summer and winter holiday, with a visit to Dr Nurick, the dentist, in Aylesbury. My mother always arranged our dreaded appointments 'good and early' so that they wouldn't hang over us. And they ended with a glorious double treat, in London.

Opera Fever

Wir wandelten durch Feuergluten,
bekämpften mutig die Gefahr,

sing Tamino and Pamina ('we pass through the heat of the fire, conquering danger with courage'), and each time I hear Schikaneder's words, I hug them, knowing how they also describe my own trial and baptism by fire.

One of my father's colleagues in the Music Department of the BBC was Leonard Isaacs. He had two children, Naomi and Nicky, and when we were nine my father and Leonard hit on the idea of initiating their four children into opera together.

Some parents would have thought a cautious 'toe in the water' approach appropriate. A jolly evening with the local operatic company, maybe. Or Gilbert and Sullivan. Or even Humperdinck. Not my father and Leonard!

On a Tuesday morning in late August, my father started BTM812 with the winder (always hazardous as it had a kick so vicious it could break your arm, or so my mother told me) and drove us up to London. Only a couple of weeks before, he and my mother had attended a Royal Garden Party and they reported that the crowd outside the gates, grown weary of a procession of Daimlers and Rolls-Royces and the like, had given our battered old car, and its abbreviated buttocks, a modest cheer as it entered the palace courtyard.

By the time we reached the Isaacs's house in north London, the car was so hot that, after my father turned off the engine, I could hear the water in the radiator gurgling and singing to itself.

The day was very hot and damp too. I stood in the quiet street, and around me everything seemed to tremble.

After lunch, Leonard led Naomi and me into his music room – Sally and Nicky were deemed too young for this part of our initiation. Leonard sat us down on either side of the piano and my father positioned himself behind it. Then the two of them introduced us to *Carmen* from start to finish, now and then warbling or breaking into a torrid duet, now and then play-acting and waving their arms. I don't think I ever saw my father more animated.

As soon as the long playthrough came to an end, Naomi and Nicky and Sally and I were ushered upstairs to rest – each in a separate room.

Then, in the early evening, the two men of music and their children ate a light early supper, and set off for Sadler's Wells.

True, I'd been to the Carlton cinema in Princes Risborough two or three times (once to see Danny Kaye in *A Song is Born*), and that had a glitzy organ; and I'd gone to several provincial pantomimes, including *Red Riding Hood*, at which I was scared whenever the wolf left the stage and kept asking when he would be coming back – when he was in view, I could at least keep an eye on him; but I had never stepped inside a theatre remotely like this.

Like the car radiator earlier in the day, I was overheated by the time I arrived, and the passionate music, and Naomi sitting next to me, only made things worse. I talked so much I must have wrecked the performance for the people sitting around me, and several times my father sternly told me to pipe down.

When, at the end of the opera, José confesses that he has

stabbed his beloved Carmen, and throws himself on to her life-less body, Naomi burst into hot tears, and couldn't stop crying. Sally thought this display of emotion was altogether excessive and highly embarrassing; I thought it was rather wonderful.

When I was twenty or thereabouts, I went to the Golders Green Hippodrome with a girl called Caroline, only just arrived in London, who had never before left her home in the Outer Hebrides. She was seventeen.

The curtains swished back to reveal the set and the actors standing on the stage – I can't remember what the play was – and Caroline sat bolt upright and very, very still. She didn't take her eyes off the stage for one moment.

After a while, she turned to me, eyes shining, and put her mouth to my right ear.

'Are they real?' she whispered.

That's how I felt at *Carmen*. I had been given a glimpse of an intense, brightly lit otherworld, that existed in tandem with my own.

Intoxicated by this heady brew of wonder, excitement, priv-ilege, passion, music, I fell asleep in the back of the car, leaning against Naomi, and I remember thinking her luscious dark hair smelt soapy.

While the four of us were blearily sipping orange juice in the Isaacs's kitchen before going to bed, my father and Leonard told Naomi and me to sleep well and for as long as we liked because they had a big surprise: the two of us were to go to the opera the next evening as well!

'*Die Zauberflöte*,' my father said. 'The Magic Flute.'

'At Covent Garden,' added Leonard.

So, the following afternoon, the whole process was repeat-ed. First, lunch in the garden; then a protracted playthrough; a short rest and a light supper; and then the journey in the ever-obliging Morris Ten, this time to the Royal Opera House.

> '*O Isis und Osiris schenket*
> *der Weisheit Geist dem neuen Paar,*'

commands the High Priest Sarastro. 'Send the spirit of wisdom to the young couple.' And again: '*Lasst sie der Prüfung Früchte sehen* . . . Let them see the fruits of their trial.'

The fruits of this overdose could, I suppose, have been to put me off opera for the remainder of my life. But, in fact, it had precisely the opposite effect. There and then I caught opera-fever, and I will never recover.

My father and Leonard were evidently well pleased with their endeavours, and began to talk about the possibility of driving us up to the Edinburgh Festival with them the following summer. My father told me that it might involve an overnight drive from Scotland back to Whiteleaf.

This was what really excited me. I kept thinking about how Naomi and I would have a rug over our laps, to help us get to sleep, and how I would be able to hold her hand, without anyone knowing, for hundreds of miles.

I was nine; and Naomi was little more than an occasional friend. But we had shared Sadler's Wells and Covent Garden, together we had thrilled to the music, and my testosterone was beginning to sing.

Singing Lessons

My parents continued to send me to Lady Mede until I was nine because they were uncertain where to send me next. Given sufficient funds, my mother would have had no compunction in despatching me to a boarding preparatory school a couple of years before, there to pick daisies in the outfield, and feel homesick, and learn self-reliance. After all, her parents had sent her away when she was only a little older, first to Northfield School in Watford where her great-aunt was head-mistress and she was the only girl (and captain of the football team), and then to Wycombe Abbey. Above all, she associated boarding schools with company, with friendships that lasted all her life.

One such was with my godmother, Mary Bridgman Shaw (née Glenn), at whose wedding I had been a two-year-old page. When I was nine, Mary went out to join her husband in Nepal, where he was Colonel-in-Chief of the Gurkhas, before the beginning of her son Mark's new school year. My mother undertook to drive Mark to his school, and the three of us saw my godmother off from Liverpool Street Station.

On the platform, she shook her eight-year-old son's right

hand, and fixed him with a warm, firm gaze. 'Now, Mark,' she said. 'Be a man.'

Not a hug; not a kiss; nothing. Even I, unused to public displays of affection, was quite shocked.

So when my parents sent me as a day-boy to Prestwood Lodge – a curious hybrid, a private school that prepared many of its children for secondary state school – it was largely *faute de mieux*. It was a holding operation, since I was too old to remain any longer at Lady Mede, while they worked out what to do.

I think I have suppressed my memories of Prestwood, and the little I do recall is wholly unpleasant. I remember ripping my grey pullover and then my shorts on a barbed-wire fence and knowing how furious my mother would be; I remember being bombarded by snowballs with small, sharp stones inside them, and being scared to death; I remember passing the preliminary Eleven Plus paper only to fail the main exam, which meant that I would not in any case be able to proceed to Aylesbury Grammar School, an outcome my parents had contemplated with no great enthusiasm and never discussed with me.

I remember, too, my relief when I contracted mumps during the summer term. Uncomfortable as they were, swollen glands were infinitely preferable to dog-days and bullies at Prestwood.

I expect I've dramatised the worst and forgotten the humdrum. Memory of one's childhood does tend to polarise in this way. But it's clear that I was unpopular to begin with, and the headmaster's report at the end of my first term speaks of 'a most distracting term . . . later on he got much better with the others and his work began to settle down'. I was a late newcomer, over-eager and anxious, who talked too much, and Prestwood was altogether more rough and tough than any school I had previously attended.

As my first term wore on, my father began to give me singing lessons each weekend, with a view to my winning a Choral Scholarship to Saint George's, Windsor, which provided the choir for the Chapel Royal. This must have been in direct response to seeing how unsettled I was at Prestwood, and to seeing my mother tearing her hair out at being unable to find a suitable alternative; I don't think it had been part of my parents' plan all along.

As my father was away in London all week, my weekend lessons were long and intensive. I stood beside the Ibach baby grand to the right of my father, and the hymns I sang, or tried to sing, are tarred with the same brush as my days at Prestwood.

In particular, I never hear more than a couple of bars of Hymn 106 in the *English Hymnal* without feeling a sense of strain, and of knowing that, hard as I tried, I was disappointing my gentle, determined teacher's expectations:

> There is a green hill far away,
> Without a city wall,
> Where the dear Lord was crucified
> Who died to save us all.

'Again and again,' my mother told me, 'you used to come out of the study with a face as white as chalk. Now if the scholarship had been for effort . . .'

A few days before Christmas, my father drove me to Windsor. There, I was shown into a large oak-panelled sitting-room where a number of men were ensconced in deep leather armchairs, the kind so inviting to relax into and almost impossible to get out of, while an accompanist awaited me at the grand piano.

The choirmaster did stand up, though. He led me across to the accompanist, and asked me what I had brought to sing.

The windows were heavily leaded; the fire was crackling in the great hearth.

Once more I sang the Passiontide hymn. I've just turned up W. Horsley's melody and, to my surprise, it consists almost entirely of quavers. In my memory it is forlorn, attenuated and dismal, nothing but minims and semibreves.

What else did I sing? Certainly not 'The Holly and the Ivy'! Rather, 'Praise the Lord! ye heavens adore him' to the valiant, cheerful melody Haydn first used in his Emperor String Quartet. Now adopted as the German national anthem, only 'La Marseillaise' and '*Hen Wlad Fy Nhadau*: Land of my Fathers' (of other national anthems) can rival its clarion call and sheer strength of purpose, and despite being obliged to sing it until I was almost hoarse, I have always loved it.

The examiners thanked me and I took my leave. Then my father drove us home.

That evening, the choirmaster telephoned my father. Saint George's, he said, were very sorry but they found themselves unable to offer me a choral scholarship; they did wonder whether perhaps I had a sore throat!

However, continued the examiner, he and the other examiners would like my parents to know how impressed they were with my manners.

'After he'd sung, he came round to each of us. He shook us each by the hand, and wished us "Happy Christmas!"'

So after Christmas, there was nothing for it. It was back through the leafless beechwoods to school at Prestwood Lodge.

I was almost ten, and my future looked very bleak.

My Museum

In the small top-garden at Crosskeys, an area little larger than a tennis court, stood a garden shed stuffed with rusty bikes, chipped flowerpots, old tins of paint, and all the other things that find their way into garden sheds.

I coveted that place. And I wanted it for a good reason.

One day, my mother went up to the gooseberry bushes behind the shed, and was shocked to find a row of seven dead chickens, laid out as neatly as petunias in a municipal border, some with their legs sticking up.

My parents had already received complaints from neighbours about Bruce, but this offence was of a different order. One of the chickens was trussed and hung around his neck, and all day my lovely bull terrier ploughed around, unable to shake off his memento.

My mother wouldn't remove the chicken, not until dusk.

'He'll never do it again,' I said. 'You won't, will you, Bruce?'

Bruce wagged his stump of a tail. Unrepentant, his eyes gleamed.

As dictated by my mother, I took Bruce out on a lead to do his business. Then Sally and I went over to the shed and, to cheer him up, we opened an old tin of paint green as the greenest grass, and painted him all over with green spots.

Bruce fairly bounded back into the house.

My mother was appalled.

Sally had to restrain Bruce while I rubbed turpentine substitute into all the spots and even then the green paint only partly came out; after this, my mother cut more of it out with scissors. Gratified at being the subject of so much attention and tender loving care, Bruce grinned and stretched out to sleep.

It was during my last term at Lady Mede, when I was nine, that my father finally agreed to let me take over the garden shed.

He and I cleared it out together and, with bricks and planks of wood, henched the far wall with simple shelves. Then we carried round from the lean-to a pair of old wooden tables and a stool.

My museum!

Irrespective of the circumstances in which children grow up, we make for ourselves (and sometimes in the least appetising, most improbable places) secret and healing retreats, where actuality and imagination meet, and time stands outside the door. And what goes on in these places is often so potent, so resonant that we revisit them for the remainder of our lives.

My climbing-tree in the glade behind Whiteleaf Cross, and the copse at Lady Mede where my friends and I held our covert meetings, a colour-loft, a backwater in the Norfolk saltmarshes: yes to each one of these, but above all yes to my museum.

Here, I laid out my treasures. On one table was my Constantine, surrounded by the nest of coins Sally had bought from the chemist in Princes Risborough, and also by my growing collection of bun pennies. I was very proud of these, and wasted a lot of time polishing them with Duraglit and trying to restore them to their pristine brightness. On one shelf were Iron Age potsherds I'd picked up with my father on Bledlow Ridge; on another were the fossils I'd found in the disused chalk-pit beneath the Cross. Beside them I placed a simple diagrammatic drawing, carefully labelled in purple ink, 'WHITE-LEAF CROSS – ONCE A FALLIC SYMBOL'. I had no idea precisely what this meant, and my parents made no attempt to enlighten me.

Then three things happened.

The first was that my father began to add items to the museum – several medieval tiles, ancient sky-blue scarabs, beads from Ur, a whole box of Iron Age coarseware from Bledlow Ridge; these and ores, some glittering, some dully gleaming; pieces of coral; prismatic glass; a hunk of Blue John, big as my fist. I added each of them to my museum catalogue, and identified each on a little strip of yellow card.

The second thing was that, when I told people about the museum, they wanted to come and see it. It soon dawned on me that this could be a valuable source of income and, without permission or telling my parents, I brought a blackboard home from Lady Mede on the bus.

One Sunday, after lunch, I went out and picked up a piece of chalk (there were always plenty by the roadside) and wrote on the board, 'MUSEUM – ENTRANCE FREE' and, below it, a bold arrow. Then I propped up the board at the top of Westfield Road, retreated and waited to see what would happen.

Some people on their Sunday outings were deflected by this sign from the steep lane leading up under the Cross, and found affixed to the gate of our cottage an altogether smaller notice, a piece of white paper with the words 'Museum – entrance one penny'.

Not everyone was deterred by this shameless petty deception. My very first visitor, who lived in Whiteleaf, astonished me by dropping into my till, an oval-shaped but actually octagonal solid lead box, painted black and burgundy and surmounted by a negro's head, two shillings-and-sixpence. Half-a-crown!

This visitor was Rumer Godden, and the second, Jacob (Bruno) Bronowski, a family friend, was not to be outdone by

Rumer and gave me the same amount. Two-and-sixpence was double my weekly pocket money, and for a fortnight I was in clover!

Then my parents discovered what I was up to; they allowed me to leave the blackboard at the top of the road, but made me take down the notice on the gate, and forbade me to charge an entry fee.

The third thing that happened was that several people presented objects to the museum.

I am holding in my right hand a long-necked Roman oil- or perfume-flask, made of slightly misty blue-green glass. Its little onion bulb has the most wonderful, lustrous, silver-and-violet patina. This flask was given to me by a woman who had retired to Whiteleaf after working for years at a museum in Egypt; it was found in the desert near Alexandria and, until I ill-advisedly washed it out, it always shed a few sandgrains when I tipped it up.

Friends brought me fossils, knapped flints, foreign coins. Then, at the end of our annual visit to Norfolk, my grandfather told me he had two gifts for my museum, both of them bought from Baker's, the great antique rooms in Fakenham – this at a time when it was still possible to find such wonders locally and even to buy them at bargain prices.

Grandpa Frank led me out across the courtyard to his *atelier*, which was a kind of pocket-sized, mock-medieval hall. In one corner was a complete suit of armour made for the Eglinton tournament of 1839; the high windows boasted sundry coats-of-arms brought from Oakwell Park. In the middle of the room stood an oak refectory table, and lying on it was a helmet and breastplate. Next to it, stretched out on one of Neenie's metal hangers, was a rusty coat-of-mail.

'They are medieval,' my grandfather told me. 'And they're for your museum.'

Then he led me through the sliding door to his small, meticulously neat, carpentry workshop. On the bench lay a shield. It too was very rusty.

'Clean it up,' Grandpa Frank said. 'Work at it. Polish it. You never know.'

Back at Whiteleaf, I proudly stood up my helmet and breast-plate on a table and hung my coat-of-mail from a hook beside the museum door. Then I set about my shield with my jack-knife and metal-wire like a barbarian, and enlisted friends to help me.

Around the shield's rim there appeared scimitars, like new moons, and a host of stars. Furiously we scrubbed, and out of the middle of the shield emerged a glaring, scowling, musta-chioed face . . .

I was electrified and, before long, my father took the shield and the helmet-and-breastplate and coat-of-mail to the Royal Armouries, then at the Tower of London, to find out more about them.

The coat-of-mail and the helmet-and-breastplate were English, and probably fourteenth century. The shield was Saracen, twelfth or early thirteenth century. How it made its way to England is unknown. It may well have been brought back by a Crusader.

Just as there are certain places, there are also crucial, revela-tory moments, akin to Gibbon's in the Forum in Rome . . . The first time that fearsome Saracen angrily stared at me, assailed me, was one of them.

A short postscript. When I was eleven, Grandpa Frank lent but did not give me another object for the museum: a broad-shouldered coarseware pot, rather ragged at the rim, undeni-ably handsome. He had bought this at Baker's too, but no one could tell him its date or provenance.

What I especially liked about this pot was the design round its shoulders: it looked as if its maker had repeatedly impressed her (or his) forefinger on to it. But when? And where? Not even Martin Jope, archaeologist and friend of my father, was able to say.

When Grandpa Frank died, my father invited me to select something in his memory. Dithering and finally turning my back on his highly desirable typewriter that worked perfectly well if one tucked a book under the right-hand side and typed uphill, I chose the coarseware pot.

Some years later, I invited to dinner Rupert Bruce-Mitford, Keeper of British and Medieval Antiquities at the British Museum, renowned for his great excavation at Sutton Hoo. Rupert brought with him his daughter Myrtle, carrying in a canvas bag the second reconstruction of the Sutton Hoo lyre, and after dinner (as befits an 'after-dinner harp') she played it.

Rupert spied my grandfather's pot, sitting quietly on a deep shelf.

'Where did you get that from?' he asked.

I explained.

'That's one of the missing pots from Spong Hill,' Rupert said.

'Where?'

'Norfolk. 1954. A burial urn, of course.'

'Anglo-Saxon?' I asked hesitantly.

'Early fifth century.'

Reverently I gazed at my pot.

'Can I have it?' asked Rupert.

I looked at him in consternation. 'You can . . . measure it . . .' I faltered. 'And borrow it. But . . . well, it's cradled by thousands of children in schools I visit.'

Rupert shuddered and closed his eyes.

I had spent the previous four years translating *Beowulf* and many of the Anglo-Saxon shorter poems. It seemed nothing short of poetic justice that this sturdy Anglo-Saxon pot should for a little while remain in my hands.

'Where beth they, beforen us weren?'

'Honour thy father and thy mother . . .'

Grandpa Frank concerned himself with establishing the family tree – some branches did have Holland blood flowing in their veins, but some were artificial limbs – and my father continued the research into our family history and documented it with impeccable scholarship.

From them I often heard about my verifiable and more shadowy ancestors. My father presented me when I was twenty-one with my own signet ring, complete with two lions rampant, and my grandfather explained that the two crosses signified the two Hollands who had been bishops while the coveted Tau Cross was awarded to the Holland who fought bravely at the Battle of Agincourt. How much all this mattered to Grandpa Frank is evident from the self-aggrandising but also self-mocking (well, I hope it was) remark he made to my parents when he first saw me lying in my cot, just a few weeks old: 'Do you realise,' he said, 'he is the scion of an armigerous family?'

It seems that my mother's family, meanwhile, were somewhat selective in whom they honoured, admiring and gently laughing at some, but quietly hiding others away.

My mother liked famous last words – the trenchant, amusing ones – and she was fond of gravestones that used wit to spike suffering, or in a few pithy words pointed to deeply held family affection and honour.

Her own mother, Mary Collard, was ninth of ten children, by no means unusual in Victorian England.

'In the same village she grew up in,' my mother told me, 'there was a family with twenty-two children. They could play a cricket match, complete with umpires, without inviting anyone to tea.'

This struck me as quite marvellous.

Sally and I were fascinated by our clan of great-uncles and great-aunts, only one of whom (Uncle Bertie) we had met, and often asked my mother to tell us about them.

My mother's eyes lightened. 'Katie, Flossie, Lily, Maud . . .' she began, as if she were winding herself up, and then the three of us together rattled off at top speed, 'Katie, Flossie, Lily, Maud, Tom, Dick, Arthur, Bertie, Mary, Jack.'

Katie and Jack, the oldest and the youngest, emigrated to Canada and to New Zealand, where the Collard Vineyard near Auckland flourished until a couple of years ago. I have in front of me the little Bible that belonged to Mary, the maternal grandmother I never met, in which she has pasted little strips from *The Times* announcing family births, marriages and deaths. Katie was married in Winnipeg cathedral . . . Mrs Jack Collard had a son . . . 'Both well,' the announcement says, terse as an old telegram. The second daughter, Flossie (or Florence), never married; she was a schoolteacher in Northamptonshire. Lily and Maud: the elder died of pneumonia aged twenty-eight while the younger died of typhoid after drinking stagnant water while bicycling in Ireland. She was twenty-six.

Arthur, too, died young; he was only twenty-three when he caught enteric fever while serving in South Africa with the 33rd Company (Royal East Kent) Imperial Yeomanry.

My mother pointed out these far-flung places on her most

exquisite double-hemisphere silk map of the world stitched by Eliz: Golby and dated Sep. 29. 1785. On the other side of the Western or Atlantic Ocean, modern Canada is divided into New Britain to the north and Canada to the south, the two stretching less than halfway across the North American continent; New Zealand is indeed New Zealand but Australia is New Holland, while South Africa is Caffreria.

But why did I hear next to nothing about the two eldest sons, Tom and Dick? Is it because one was a cripple, and one shot himself? And what does that say about honour? Did my mother really know next to nothing about them, as she professed, or did she elect to show her young children ambition and achievement and to pass lightly over suffering and shame?

Her favourite uncle was certainly Bertic, a bluff, successful fruit-farmer with a splendid shock of white hair. He reciprocated her feelings, and several times entertained my mother, Sally and me at his farm, near Liss in Hampshire.

What I especially liked about our visits were the vast number of horse-brasses hung along the oak beams in the sitting room; the haybarn for romping; those and, of course, the strawberry fields where we were allowed to pick and eat as we liked.

Each year, a few women, usually young and glamorous, have a flower named after them. The Darcey Bussell rose, crimson fading to pale purple, recently made her curtsy at the Chelsea Flower Show. My mother's uncle Bertie, owner of the then largest fruit-farm in Hampshire, named one species of strawberry 'Joan' after his favourite niece.

The dominions, and North America only newly independent; three children struck down with typhoid and pneumonia and enteric fever; depression and physical disability hidden well out of sight . . . I keep looking at Eliz: Golby's map, its gold and burgundy outlines, the dotted black lines indicating 'Cook's Track', its black place names. Moscovy and Eastern Tartary, the Desert of Barbary, Negroland . . . What was the distance from 1785 until, say, 1900? And how far from 1900 to today?

Making Magic

Children sometimes ask me whether any episodes in my novels are autobiographical, and of course the answer is both yes and no. That's to say I can point to dozens and dozens of characters and conversations and dilemmas and moments of wonder rooted in my childhood, but I use those years as a quarry and trigger, not as a photographic negative.

In *The Seeing Stone*, for instance, I wrote a couple of pages in which I tried to distil many conversations I had with my father about degrees of magic: God's magic; the power inherent in some words and non-lexical sounds; herbs and drugs; and conjuring tricks.

A quest for wisdom and a certain childlikeness and playfulness are not incompatible; on the contrary, they often go hand in hand.

My father had a repertoire of simple conjuring tricks, loving them no less for their absurdity than for the way in which they expose time and reason for the impostors they are, and he unselfconsciously showed them off whenever there was a decent opportunity to do so.

Sitting at the kitchen table, Sally and I marvelled when

Tinker Bell danced in through the window and flitted round the room, alighting on the Aga, and on Jamini Roy's painting of three Indian fishermen, a christening present to Sally from her godfather Adrian Cruft, and then trembling on her outstretched palm.

My father covered his right hand with a white handkerchief and with his left hand slowly uncovered it . . . Up! Up! The tension was almost unbearable. And what did he reveal? His thumb! His thumb, sticking up to heaven, and four fingers curled into his palm.

Then he passed a coin from one hand to another and made it disappear; he discovered stones or lumps of plasticine in our ears. *Homo ludens . . .*

Sally and I adored these tricks, and my father's fondness for them never diminished. His grandchildren all referred to them, and to their own sense of wonder and delight, in a booklet of memories compiled for his seventieth birthday.

Although my parents responded to my urgent pleas and more than once gave me a box of conjuring tricks for my birthday or Christmas, I discovered my prescribed tricks were a poor substitute for my father's inspired improvisation.

Amongst my parents' far-flung friends – those who vanished for years at a time and then mysteriously appeared on the doorstep – were a small, jokey Lancashire man, Eric Rodgers, and his busty wife Olive, an opera singer, who nonplussed but also impressed me by telling me that she always gave presents to her family and friends on her own birthday.

My father and Eric set one another off, each performing for each other, and making magic for Sally and me. To begin with, these were simple tricks, not feats such as the *Tain*'s 'juggling nine apples, and the spurt of speed, and the snapping mouth, and the stepping on a flying lance, and the stunning shot, and the salmon-leap' that I shamelessly magpied and incorporated into *The Seeing Stone*.

But then Eric picked up a pole more than twice as long as he was; I think my father was using it to edge one of his vegetable beds.

With some difficulty, but maybe not as much as he made us believe, Eric raised the pole upright, lifted it, and then balanced it on his right forefinger.

Round the garden he shuffled, never for one moment taking his eyes off the top of the pole, and excitedly I danced backwards in front of him, like a little Will Kemp of the Chilterns.

'How do you do it?' I asked Eric afterwards. 'How do you do it?'

Eric thrust up his chin and raised his eyes.

Children well know that there is only a wavy dividing line between the actual and the imaginary, and that a lumpen cloud may well be an angry face and the tasselled dressing-gown hanging on the back of the bedroom door may well be tigerish. They still relish sheer trickery.

I hopped and I jigged, I tripped and fell backwards into a flowerbed, feet in the air, laughing.

Phew!

Dissatisfaction and a sense of hurt tend to feed on themselves. Day by day I grew more unhappy at Prestwood Lodge and this, taken with my failure of the Eleven Plus exam and inability to win a place at Saint George's, Windsor, confronted my parents with a difficult problem.

It was at this point that one or other of them had the idea of sending me to the heavily subsidised Christ's Hospital. They made contact with a presentation governor and I duly took the entrance exam during March 1951. This I passed, and the school offered me a place for September. But almost immediately, my father's salary at the BBC increased to a level at which I was no longer eligible for subsidised fees. Since there was no question of my parents being able to afford the full fees, it was back to square one again.

But challenges are just what my mother liked. She contacted and then went to see an old friend from her tennis-playing days, Harold Evans, now the owner-headmaster of Swanbourne House Preparatory School, only a few miles from Mursley where I was born.

My mother threw herself on Mr Evans's mercy, telling him

how unhappy I was and concerned she was, explaining that she and my father were unable to afford the full fees of sixty guineas per term, at least in the first instance, then asking whether he could nonetheless find a place for me.

Mr Evans's response was immediate and generous. 'I'll put up a camp bed for him, if need be.'

So in September 1951, I went to Swanbourne. Aged ten, I was a couple of years older than all the other new boys, but I was a 'squit' all the same, and thus had to perform inelegant but harmless initiation rites, such as dancing on a desk-top in front of the jeering top form or 'set' as we called it, and running up and down the forbidden, slippery Front Stairs. I was also subjected to a couple of doses of mild bullying by an older boy with the splendidly Dickensian name of Grummett. He used to lock my arm in a half-Nelson and twist it until I begged for mercy; but my humiliation never amounted to more than that.

It felt very strange but not unduly troubling to step into a world where I would not see or speak to Sally or my parents until quarter-term, three weeks ahead, and where no one at all

SWANBOURNE HOUSE · SCHOOL

'I'll put up a camp bed for him, if need be.'

used my Christian name. As it happened, a boy called Holland had left the school at the end of the previous term. Because of his badly pocked face, he had been nicknamed Morbus; so, naturally, I inherited his name.

It is so easy to parody or demonise mid-century preparatory and public schooling, and plenty of writers have taken shots at it, many of them cheap. The truth, of course, is more complex. There were some bad apples, just as there were and are bad state schools, and such a robust system certainly taxes some sensibilities; but to my mind its assets easily outweigh its defects.

More than fifty years ago, the philosophy of sink or swim, and a score-based, competition-conscious system was more pronounced than it is now. It didn't take me long to discover that I was rather below average in almost every subject, without quite being bottom of the class.

The subjects that most interested me were, predictably, history and geography, though I found the geography master's withering tongue almost impossible to take. Most children are rendered helpless and feel extremely vulnerable when confronted by sarcasm. Perhaps the only subject in which I knew I excelled was, as at Lady Mede, mental arithmetic. I have never had much difficulty in adding, subtracting, multiplying, dividing in my head. But at Swanbourne, sterner tests awaited me: algebra, geometry, trigonometry.

'Floppy' Wright, the master in charge of Latin and cricket, was the terror of the school. He used to tower menacingly over us, and yell, and slam our desk lids, incised with the initials of generations of pupils. Once, I incurred Floppy's serious wrath, and he hurled a whole pile of new, hardback textbooks at me, one after another. Over my head they flew, royal blue Frisbees with dangerous sharp corners, and smack-smack-smacked into the classroom wall. But this man: he knew the language spoken by the Emperor Constantine and the two soldiers on my Roman coin; and with the sweetest patience and forgiving smile that was the complete antithesis to his vile temper, he showed me how Latin would underpin my knowledge of English and French. To him, I owe part of my lifelong delight in language.

For all this, my academic progress at Swanbourne was slow. I never graduated to Set 1, who all sat scholarship exams to public schools; on the contrary, by the time I was thirteen it was still not at all certain that I would even pass my Common Entrance exam.

'You will,' said my mother. 'You'll squeak through. You're always twelfth man in a team of eleven.'

This was only partly true. Much as I loved our daily sporting activities, preceding afternoon classes in winter and spring and following them during the longer summer days, I was only sure of a first-team place in football (I played inside left). I also turned out for the rugby team when it was augmented from the First XII to the First XV against such serious opponents as Summerfields School, but I never played for the First XI at cricket.

And yet! If I were to list the eleven greatest joys of my life, one of them would be this. I am twelve or thirteen again, and it is April, and I'm sitting on a slatted bench beneath my locker in the pale grey-green changing-room at Swanbourne. The number of my locker is 29, and I'm happy that it can't be divided. It's a prime number. Around me, I can hear the firing of shots in the rifle range, flushing cisterns next door in the 'bogs', and bumping and clumping in the scout-loft overhead. But I have a job to do: I have to oil my cricket bat for the first time this season.

I open my locker, and there at the back is my sticky-and-dusty bottle of linseed oil. I pour a glob on to the top of the bat, just below the grainy V-shaped splice, and another near the bottom. Then I begin. Fingertips first. My whole left hand. Round and round in small circles, opening the pores of the willow.

The back of the bat is angled, so it's less easy to stop the succulent oil from trickling and dribbling . . . Now the front again

. . . The willow drinks. It drinks until it becomes quite plump and juicy. Then, all at once, it's saturated. Satiated. The job is done.

My fingertips, pink and tingling; the blade of the bat, mottled, surprisingly rough to the touch, bruised and abraded, with cherry echoes of blows well struck; the rubber handle, slightly sticky; and for three years, at the back of my locker, the miraculous cruse – the supply, seemingly self-replenishing, of sweet, thick, nourishing linseed oil.

There was one sport, though, that I dreaded: swimming. True, Grandpa Frank had one day offered Sally and me the princely incentive of five shillings each if we learned to swim. I learned that selfsame day, but forgot again soon after.

At Swanbourne, swimming took place immediately after cricket or athletics on each summer afternoon, but I had to return to the 'Swimming Bath' early some evenings for a swimming lesson.

The master who taught me was waiting for me, holding a stick with a length of rope attached to it. At the end of the rope was a hangman's noose. When I'd got down into the water, something I still resist, I had to slip this noose around my stomach, and then the master hoicked me off my feet, and I struck out while he very slowly paced around the rim of the pool.

I gasped and choked and got water up my nose, all the time dreading the moment when the master would lower the stick, and the rope would no longer be taut, and I would go under. Great was my pleasure when, as I wrote home, 'it was discovered I had got 2 verookas. I expect you know what they are. Anyhow, I won't be able to swim this term or anyhow till 3/4 term.'

Now? I can swim the breaststroke, like a novice, straining to keep my head above water; and I can float, just about. But I still cordially dislike swimming, and have always supposed, irrationally, that I will die by drowning.

Sink or swim! The tight, predictable brace of our

Swanbourne days left us with little time for floundering, required the good manners I'd been taught at home, and reinforced my self-reliance, self-discipline and self-confidence.

At meals, we were expected to eat what was put in front of us, every scrap of it. England was a country in which each individual and family still had a ration book, and a dim view was taken of waste.

But that didn't stop me from concealing Friday morning breakfast – poached haddock, invariably – wherever I could: under my feet, plastered to the underside of the dining table, or even in my trouser pockets.

Breakfast was immediately followed by a short service in the glassy chapel. Despite my father's best efforts, I was still unable to read music but, all the same, I was immediately given a stall in the choir. Day after day we belted out the manful and melancholy hymns that have been the staple diet of Church of England services for the last century, but what I liked most was the sense of teamwork and the slow-motion, antiphonal singing of psalms.

We didn't wear surplices but were expected to look well groomed. I was used to that – early each holiday, my mother used to drive me over to Oxford for 'a proper haircut' in the Turl.

Not long ago, my wife and I followed immaculately turned-out members of the American Boychoir into a university quadrangle on their way to a performance.

One boy gave his friend an almighty dig in the ribs.

'All right, Nils!' he fluted. 'Sing like the little angel you are.'

So the hours passed, each filled with prescribed classes and activities; while on Sunday mornings we attended the service in the chapel and then wrote our weekly letter home. This had to be read and approved by the master on duty.

Those Sunday letters! They give a very fair idea of my preoccupations and manners. Evidently, I hit the ground running and in my first letter I wrote, 'I am having a wonderful time here. I hope you are not too lonely at home. Can Sally ride her bicycle yet?'

This considerate and inclusive tone is one of the *leitmotifs* of my letters. 'I am glad the car is all right now,' I wrote. 'It must have hindered your work. I hope it will not interfere with your work if you come on Wednesday.' And again: 'When Sally's and Daddy's birthdays come, tell them to look in the second top draw (*sic*) of the brown chester-drawers (*sic*).' Some of the letters contain encouraging messages for Sally: 'It is much the best writing you have ever done. Who spelt clutch for you? I will write to you soon.' But one at least is brutally frank in the way siblings are: 'You may become someone in ballet one day but you must get thinner first.'

For the most part, I was very polite ('I am terribly sorry to tell you that I looked at my watch which I keep in my pocket and one hand was off') but also robust: 'I have got such a lot to say that I don't know where to begin. I think I'll begin with your complaints Mummy. I did tell you last holiday that my cricket bat practically split down the middle and is unusable . . . Naomi has sent me a letter and I will write back to her as soon as I have time. Incidentally, I do always, always write back to people who write to me.'

Just about every letter contains brief but spirited and enthusiastic reports of the previous week's sporting fixtures, an account of the weekly film, and sundry requests – for cake, balsa wood, what I called trashes (comics) and occasionally a book: 'I've asked for a Rider Haggard book because they are almost classics.'

Sometimes my letters are unintentionally absurd in their juxtapositions or long-windedness: 'The pity about being ill in bed is I will no longer have a chance of moving up . . . It is really terrible for me to think of it.' They're packed with *frightfullys* and *terriblys* and *wizards* and *phews!* and *penalty areas*. And yet, quite often, they sound old for my age. But overall these weekly epistles are rapid, highly impressionable, properly modest, and eager. Here's one, written when I was twelve:

Dear Mummy, Daddy and Sally,

I have a lot to tell you.

First on Friday night, McDonald (Sir Ian Fraser's grandson) actually lent me his battery wireless. I heard Daddy's name mentioned, also someone Ross. I heard six snatches of the carols. I was very pleased because it was so late and it was only [a] battery wireless. I think I ought to give some present to McDonald because he risked getting his wireless confiscated and also it was so late. After the carols someone woke up with a nightmare, but it was not the carols. I told Mr Barry about the carols and he appeared to tell Mr Evans, anyhow Mr Evans listened and he said they were wizard. Also, Mr Barry told Miss Noakes and Mr Mathewson. Mr Mathewson with his usual good humour said that it was not disharmonic. He also said that Miss Noakes liked the first one very much. Barry himself liked them very much indeed.

I may be able to get some stamps for you Sally.

We had our photographs taken on Wednesday, the picture of me has come out very well.

Yesterday we won the 2nd XI match and drew the first XI. We have only lost two this season.

It was lovely last Sunday going out and the time seems to be going quickly now.

Longing to see you again

Love
Kevin

On Sunday afternoons at Swanbourne, we at last had time for ourselves. I photographed an eclipse of the sun through a piece of darkened glass; I bowled in the nets or played cricket against the courtyard wall; with friends, I badmouthed the headmaster's daughter, and dreamed of lashing her to one of the vast, crumbling Wellingtonias, there to languish until dusk; I did my viola practice; I wandered along wooded paths, some safe, some conducive to ambushes, quickly making inroads on the 2½ oz of sweets we were allowed to select after lunch each Sunday, and that were put on the scales and measured out with weights by Matron (sweets were rationed in England until 1953); I booked my turn in the rifle range; I began to feel a little but never unduly homesick . . .

We were allowed 'out' three times each term: twice for a Sunday, once for a whole weekend.

BTM812 was almost invariably the first car through the gates, and this mattered so much to me that, when I later sent my sons to preparatory school, I was often early and never once late, even when for two years I had to travel each month from Germany. My mother then drove me rapidly back to Whiteleaf, a journey of about eighteen miles, and there Sally and my father and Bruce and a handsome lunch awaited me.

There's nothing like deprivation to sharpen appreciation. Those hours were very precious, and I saw the familiar with new eyes: tadpoles in the pond, wild strawberries in the upper field, the little alpine plants snug in the rockery, the bed of red hot pokers, the greengage tree, my museum . . .

During my second half-term, I got flu, and my mother despatched me to bed. There, on my transistor radio – a square dark-blue box that opened like a vanity case, I listened to a rugby international between England and Ireland. I don't know why, perhaps because I'd seen the magical Jackie Kyle playing for Major Stanley's XV against Oxford, perhaps because my mother had Irish blood in her veins, but I found myself guiltily supporting Ireland. Hot and hoarse, I shuddered; my temperature rose to 104°; I had to stay at home for a further week.

But yes! Jackie Kyle excelled himself, Ireland won 6–3. And through thick and thin, I have supported Ireland ever since.

On another outing, the fog came down just as my mother and I were about to set off for Swanbourne and, after nosing halfway to Aylesbury, my mother abruptly gave up and turned for home. That evening, everything seemed like a gift: the minced meat and floury potatoes; the little box of indoor fireworks Sally and I set off in the hearth, one by one.

After my very first outing from Swanbourne, I pressed my mother to stay for Sunday evensong. First she said no. Then, against her better instincts, she said yes. After all, strong-minded and unsentimental as she was, she was the same woman who some years before had heard me confiding to Sally: 'Mummy will do anything if you force her to.'

My mother stood near the back of the congregation and I took my place in the choir. Then Mr Evans, who looked almost as much like a giraffe as a human, announced 'Hymn 25. The day Thou gavest . . .'

'The day Thou gavest, Lord, is ended . . .' The one day between now and half-term, three whole weeks ahead. Almost one month.

As I sang, my throat tightened, my eyeballs grew hot, and then two fat tears lolloped onto my hymnbook.

Later, I sneaked a look at my mother, and she smiled and nodded. Her eyes were bright with tears. And she never stayed for evensong again.

So am I whistling in the dark? For all Swanbourne's undoubted assets, was I more lonely than I remember? Not so, according to my weekly letters.

Swept up in the Dance

Think where man's glory most begins and ends,
And say my glory was I had such friends.

W. B. Yeats's stirring couplet is all very well, but it speaks of
adulthood and implies choice. You cannot tell so much about
a child from the friends he or she makes because they're quite
likely to have been visited or even foisted upon him by siblings,
by parents or circumstance.

There was just one house standing between Crosskeys and
Whiteleaf Cross, and this belonged to the Bromleys. Stephen
and Martin were several years younger than me but, because
they lived over the fence, I quite often played games in the garden with them, as well as resolving to become a diplomat after
talking to their inspiring Foreign Office father, and once playing a curiously intense game of cards *à deux* with their mother
– so intense, in fact, that I decided to lose, something I've only
once done since, except when loosening the reins while playing
with my children when they were still young.

Home from Swanbourne with newly acquired footballing
skills, I showed them off by dribbling between Diana
Bromley's meticulous flower-beds, and teaching Stephen and

Martin how to tackle properly, and the like. Little Stephen was so elastic that he seemed to fall over and stand up again all in one movement; I remember thinking he was like a self-righting manikin.

Shortly after we left Crosskeys and moved to London, when I was seventeen, we heard the most appalling news. Diana Bromley, who was a niece of the horror-film actor Boris Karloff, had carried her sleeping sons out to their car in their pyjamas, and reversed the exhaust system, and asphyxiated them. Then she cut their throats and tried to cut her own as well. Neighbours found her wandering in the garden, sobbing.

Those words in the funeral service: 'In the midst of life we are in death': remembering Stephen and Martin, and reviewing the depleted ranks of my childhood friends, I recognise the truth of them. There are two short passages in the Anglo-Saxon elegies that matter a great deal to me. One is a passionate celebration of a human being's insatiable hunger for life; the other, in 'The Wanderer', is a powerful and mournful meditation on arbitrary fate and on transience:

> Where has the horse gone? Where the man? Where the
>   giver of gold?
> Where is the feasting-place? And where the pleasures of
>   the hall?
> I mourn the gleaming cup, the warrior in his corselet,
> the glory of the prince. How that time has passed away,
> darkened under the shadow of night as if it had never been
>   . . .
> Nothing is ever easy in the kingdom of earth,
> the world beneath the heavens is in the hands of fate.
> Here possessions are fleeting, here friends are fleeting,
> here man is fleeting, here kinsman is fleeting,
> the whole world becomes a wilderness.

In Whiteleaf, there were some twenty children, and with a shock I realise that no fewer than five of them died young: not only Stephen and Martin, but Robert, who lived with us in

London for a while, and threw himself off a bridge; and Mary and Pat, Sally's two best friends, who both died of cancer.

The Findlays and the Crossley-Hollands, the Crossley-Hollands and the Findlays: ours was a friendship not only between individuals but between families that began more than sixty years ago and is still flourishing.

In my mother's carefully selected and captioned photograph albums, there are many snaps of the three Findlay children, Ann, Christopher and Geoffrey. Wearing her trademark white pinafore dress, Ann, a couple of months older than me – and try as I may, I've never quite caught her up – looks levelly and intelligently and capably into the camera. The five of us were at Lady Mede together, and Ann was top of the class while Christopher was a notably good actor. I remember he played the giant in the school's production of *Jack the Giant-Killer*, and stomped around the hollow performing-platform on blocked shoes, wearing a high hat and declaiming 'Fee! Fi! Fo! Fum! I smell the blood of an Englishman.'

Like Sally and me, the Findlays had a dressing-up box, and Christopher enjoyed wearing girls' clothes, something encouraged by his mother (who dressed him up as a girl to go to fancy-dress parties), but by ours found unnatural and distasteful.

The Findlay children also had an enviable toy theatre, complete with curtains that swept across the front of the little stage. They made magic in their own sitting room.

Geoffrey, a couple of years younger than Sally, was my mother's spirited godson. When I was nine and Geoffrey five, our families had a tea-party under the greengage tree in the garden at Crosskeys. Geoffrey started leaping up and down. Before long, he landed on my mother's wooden tray, and his feet went right through it. Geoffrey's mother was worried in case he'd got splinters; my mother just laughed; I felt indignant that she wasn't cross with him, as she certainly would have been with me.

Sally and I spent a good deal of time with the Findlays,

though they had little of my love of sport. Theirs was a home from home, and on one occasion, Sally, aged four, decided to show them our new kitten.

The telephone rang at the bottom of the stairs in Crosskeys, and my mother answered it.

'Are you short of a daughter?' asked the disembodied voice. Sally had simply picked up the kitten, cradled it and set off for Red Roofs, the Findlays' house, three-quarters of a mile away. My mother had no idea she was missing.

Philip Findlay was a distinguished research scientist who worked at the Forest Products Research Laboratory, known locally as 'The Lab', and his wife Laura was one of the best-read people I have met. They treated children with proper seriousness – that's to say as equals in everything but experience. They were Scottish. They were courteous, but frank.

At Crosskeys, there was music, a sense of the numinous, style, wit, and competition of all kinds; at Red Roofs, the temper was more studious. Whereas my mother read rather little, Laura was not only a serial reader, if that's the right term, but always had several books on the go at the same time. She talked of the characters in Thackeray and Dickens and George Eliot as if they were old friends.

This was a revelation. And when, aged twenty-three, I published my first novel for children, *Havelok the Dane*, and gave a copy to Laura, she wrote me a forthright, warm letter, praising me, castigating me . . . I should have expected no less. It was the first detailed critical estimate of my writing I had ever had, and in my mind it remains the most marvellous.

At Red Roofs, there was enquiry, rational discussion and scientific explanation but time, too, for sing-songs round the piano (especially of Gilbert and Sullivan), while Laura was evidently an accomplished parodist. She encapsulated her many friendly arguments with my mother in these spirited lines:

If you want a receipt for that popular mystery

Known to the world as the Spiritual Truth,
Take all the most notable teachers in history,
Search for their essence, but don't look for proof.
The science of Darwin who upturned our history,
Doctrines of Gurdjieff who thought life a dream,
Ideals of Hermes, whose life's such a mystery,
The Gospels of Jesus that Teacher supreme.
The sayings of Buddha, who's called the Enlightened One,
Poems of Shelley on beauty and truth,
Thoughts of Teresa, the saint and the holy nun,
Smatter of Rousseau, although he's uncouth.
Be wary of preaching that's too categorical;
Study some teaching that's eschatological;
Flavour of Steiner; Ouspensky a touch of him;
Dash of Mahommed, but not very much of him!
Plato and Socrates, Gandhi and Shaw,
Thomas Aquinas and some of Tagore.

Take of these elements all that is fusible,
Melt them all down in a pipkin or crucible,
Set them to simmer and take off the scum,
And the Spiritual Truth is the residuum.

The Findlays were vegetarians and furnished my mother
with all kinds of statistics to argue their case. Systematically,
they brought over French au pair girls year after year, not only
to look after Ann, Christopher and Geoffrey but to teach them
French (Geoffrey's subsequent posting as diplomat in Paris
was surely in part due to this Francophilia). But what I most
enjoyed at Red Roofs, without ever explaining it to myself,
was family. The familial spirit. The togetherness. They were a
proper family; we were not.

After spending weeks away at school, I began to relish time
with my old friends. And of course an increased awareness of
time, making good use of opportunity, accepting its limitation,
are part of the process of growing up. 'Summer's lease . . .'

Some friends were of my own choosing, such as Ann Hellings, my apple-and-paperchase-and-shotgun-pellet-partner, and the deliciously-named Sabrina Pavry, and Andy, the pilot's son, with whom I played tennis and, later, golf, and watched a cottage burn down. Some were friends of Sally's, such as Pat Mackay, with whom my sister blew pearly bubbles, and tried on dresses and dreamed endless dreams, and the more earthy Mary Lacey, who lived just across the lane.

Mary appeared at our back door. 'I strod on a worm,' she announced cheerfully.

My mother made her take off her shoes before she came into the kitchen.

Certainly, she accepted Sally's and Mary's friendship, but I see now that it went against the social grain. She was unenthusiastic about my occasional fraternising with Mary's elder brother, already at High Wycombe Grammar School, on the grounds that 'he's older than you are' and 'you've plenty of other friends already' and, more pointedly, 'he's not really from the same sort of background as you'.

There's no other word for this but snobbery, but my mother's attitude still surprises me because she was intelligent and in many respects so liberal. Not only that. Mary and Michael were the children of Winifred Beechey, later the author of a shining family memoir, *The Rich Mrs Robinson* (1984). I suppose my mother was a child of her own time and station, pragmatic not doctrinaire, but in some ways unthinking – the same sort of mix that led to a fashionable and poisonous aversion to the Jews between the wars.

Some occasional friends, meanwhile, were children of my parents' friends: the older Francis and Benedict Rubbra (sons of Edmund and Antoinette), who allowed us to feed their donkey, and the somewhat younger Lisa (now Lisa Jardine) and Judy Bronowski.

Sally and I used to sit with Lisa and Judy on the bus back from Lady Mede, and they were met by their mother, Rita, at the bus stop at the bottom of Peter's Lane.

My mother told me that on one occasion I marched into the cottage and reported, 'I saw Rita at the bus stop. She had a Labourish look on her face.'

Not long before, my mother had evidently introduced me to the political parties and their roots, and what they stood for, and told me with some distaste that Bruno and Rita voted Labour!

Friends of our choosing, sometime friends from Lady Mede, friends of friends: many were swept up, quite literally, in the dance, when my mother arranged for us to have dancing classes on Saturday mornings.

Why was I so utterly inept?

I can still hear our teacher: 'Kevin, you're going round the wrong way! Kevin, you must lead your partner! She's leading you!'

I'm physically well co-ordinated and have a decent ear, but maybe I tried too hard. As with my feeble attempts to learn the viola, anxiety and filial piety tripped me up.

Not long ago, my wife and I danced until we almost dropped at an Italian village *sagra*. I was rather pleased with my mobility, inventiveness and stamina. Then Linda congratulated me on my astonishing ability to vary the slow-quick-quick-slow of the quickstep so as to accommodate every possible dance rhythm. I was mortified!

Dance, dance . . . Andy and Anthony, and you Ann – well, you four Ann(e)s, Christine and Christopher and Edmund and Geoffrey and Graham, Ian and James and Jennifer, Judy and Karen, Lisa and Mary and Nicola and Pat and Philip and Richard and Sabrina and Sybil and Terry. I hope my alphabet of our childhood rings true. I hope you will dance, dance, in sunlight, in shade, wherever you may be.

In Norfolk: Cometh the Hour . . .

I proudly showed my collection of Victorian bun pennies to Grandpa Frank.

He looked at one of the most worn specimens through his magnifying glass.

'1840,' he said. 'You could write a letter to *The Times* about how old this one is.'

I knew better than to interrupt. Grandpa Frank didn't like the rat-a-tat-tat of quick conversation; he favoured short speeches.

My grandfather duly helped me to write a short letter. I copied it out carefully, addressed the envelope to the Editor, and affixed a 2½d stamp.

At noon a few days later Grandpa Frank stumped downstairs as usual to do 'his business' – at such times, Sally and I were confined to the other end of the house and not allowed to play in the courtyard outside the bathroom and lavatory. Then he came into the sitting room and sat down in his armchair.

'Kevin,' he said quite casually, 'I see *The Times* has printed your letter.'

A couple of days later, the paper printed another letter,

beginning 'Mr Crossley-Holland's bun penny is certainly old, but regrettably it is no longer current. The earliest valid currency was minted in 1841 . . .'

Grandpa Frank was delighted: in his Victorian eyes, children were adults-in-waiting, and with the letter I had composed and he had tutored, it was as if I had begun to validate myself.

There was one Sunday lunch at Rahere when Grandpa Frank was especially verbose. On and on he went, cleverly beginning a new sentence before inserting another mouthful so that no one could interrupt him while he was chewing – and this was all the more frustrating because Sally and I didn't want to miss the last ferry up to Scolt Head.

At last, my grandfather finished his peroration.

'Grandpa,' I leaped in. 'Um . . .'

Grandpa Frank waved his fork in the air and then pointed his knife at me accusingly. 'Did you say um?' he asked. He swallowed and his Adam's apple bobbed. 'Did I hear you say um?'

There followed an interminable homily on why it is never right to begin in a way that suggests uncertainty or lack of mastery of the language.

There was nothing for it but to suffer in silence. Sally gave me a Donald Duck look, and I lowered my head so that Grandpa Frank couldn't see I was smiling.

'You understand, Kevin?' he asked.

'Yes, Grandpa,' I said meekly.

Grandpa Frank jerked his head round and stared gimlet-eyed at Sally. 'And that goes for you too,' he said.

Poor Sally. She hadn't even got as far as opening her mouth to say anything throughout the entire meal.

My grandfather was a skilful and imaginative carpenter, and in another incarnation he would have been a good forger. Just as he had little compunction about dovetailing the verifiable and the speculative in matters of family history, he sometimes cobbled and grafted at his immaculate workbench.

I own a very slim, leggy, rectangular oak table assembled by my Grandpa Frank. At first sight it looks all of a piece. It is nothing of the sort. It is a composite, a combination of Georgian tabletop, Victorian legs and, very likely, twentieth-century struts.

My grandfather invented the Crossley Comfort, much the most comfortable and convenient piece of garden furniture I have ever sat in, with flat semi-circular arms larger than lily-pads on either side of the seat.

During the eighties, my uncle Dick's widow, Rosemary, had a copy made of the Crossley Comfort. She asked my father's permission to test out the market for it. On the absurd grounds that he might have the chair manufactured himself, he refused.

The sheer meanness of this is a sure sign of the depth of my father's resentment at the way in which he believed his parents had favoured Dick. Maybe they did. They certainly favoured me, and Sally felt it bitterly.

But what I see more and more clearly is that to understand why we have been hurt by no means necessarily prevents us from consciously or blindly inflicting precisely the same hurt on our own children. Thus my father saw but failed to grasp emotionally how badly his own lack of even-handedness hurt Sally. Because she was not intellectual, she began to think he was disappointed in her and, although he loved her, he was unable to cut to the chase and tell her so.

In his workshop, Grandpa Frank made us wonders: for Sally, a doll's house; for me, a Noah's Ark, complete with a set of cut-out, meticulously painted wooden animals; this and a windmill-and-cottage mounted at two ends of an oblong plinth, linked by a band of grey tape. When I wound the brass handle set into the plinth, Kevin Miller came out of his mill and advanced on his cottage.

But for most of our waking hours in Norfolk, Sally and I were outdoors, and that's where I collected an assortment of injuries.

We had a small, flat-bottomed boat – her name, *Mallard*, lovingly painted by my grandfather on a grey nameplate in navy-blue letters, edged with grass-green and gold. One morning, I rowed Sally a few strokes across to the islet in the middle of the creek that I called Kenwood in honour of the chocolate bars we used to eat there. Twenty or twenty-five yards at the most and very much less at low water.

There, I told Sally to stand back, and whirled my orange fishing-line around my head. I cast it, and lodged the barbed hook in the ball of my right thumb.

My blood spurted all over my hand and ran down to my elbow; I couldn't row one-handed; the grey tide was frisky . . .

Cometh the hour, cometh the girl. Sally was six and had never rowed before, but at once she marshalled me into the bows, grasped the oars and pulled us across.

In the surgery in Burnham Market, the doctor anaesthetised my hand and wiggled the hook. I watched, as if in a dream.

'I'll try just one more time,' he said.

'What if it doesn't come out?'

'I'll have to push it right through,' the doctor replied.

It came out.

But this was small beer compared to the injury I had sustained the previous year, when I was eight. It was Overy Staithe's Regatta and Water Sports Day. I was nothing like good enough to go in for any of the swimming races but had entered for the rowing race, and could scarcely wait for the tide to turn and the sports to begin.

A holiday friend and I picked up some pieces of pale-grey slate and skimmed them across what was left of the water in the creek. Then we waded around and retrieved them and positioned ourselves on opposite sides of the creek, thirty yards or so apart.

Ducks and drakes! I used to skim and chuck stones of all shapes and sizes every time we came to Norfolk, but I'd never known anything to compare with those slates. Several times, I actually skimmed one right across the creek from bank to bank.

My friend did the same. And then, standing up to my shins

21 Sally aged five, with her doll Clare

22 *Whiteleaf Woods*: a watercolour by John Nash

23 Laura Findlay, with her children Ann, Christopher (right) and Geoffrey

24 P.E. at Lady Mede – I am nearest to the camera and Karen Thomas is on my right

25 With Lisa and Judy Bronowski
26 Naomi and Nicky Isaacs
27 Laurent Gruson, with medieval helmet and breastplate
28 With my sister, and John, Polly and Sally Richter
30 Sally, you've got to score seven runs . . .

31 Gun Hill and the tidal island of Scolt Head
32 An aerial photograph of Scolt Head

32 Sally and her father examining a piece of cornelian

33 In the shallow end

34 With my father and Uncle Dick, Sally, Andrew and Jonathan (in pram)

35 With Aunt Rosemary and Uncle Dick: family picnic

36 In the Valais
37 Glacial: my parents and Sally with Bertha Milich, near Arolla
38 My parents with Neenie and Sally in north Italy

Whiteleaf Cross   Estate of Clare Leighton

39 My father at the Three Choirs Festival in Worcester
40 With Sally at Crosskeys
41 Leaving for Bryanston for the first time
42 Whiteleaf Cross by Clare Leighton (1934)

in the muddy water, I saw one of his slates skipping straight towards me. Before I could move, it sliced into my right shin, exposing a scimitar of shockingly white bone. The deep wound scarcely bled. And, to begin with, it scarcely hurt.

I walked sedately, gingerly, back to Rahere, and this time my destination was Wells Cottage Hospital.

Having had a whiff of ether more than once at the dentist in Aylesbury, I was intent on avoiding an anaesthetic at all costs.

'It's all right,' I told the doctor. 'I won't look.'

The doctor smiled sympathetically.

'I don't mind if it hurts.'

The doctor gently shook his head.

'I'll read something. I promise.'

I put up a stiff resistance, and when a nurse laid a cotton pad over my cheeks and nose before clamping the anaesthetiser over them, I tore it off and hurled it across the room. Three times.

Then two nurses crossed my arms and held me down while the third put me under.

Some while later, stitched up and groggy, I sat beside the creek in the back seat of BTM812 and watched the rowing race I had entered for. I watched the swimming races and the Greasy Pole. Then my mother drove me back to Rahere and I was violently sick.

I don't think my parents issued me with any warnings or prohibitions because of accidents such as these. They saw them as casualties of childhood's battleground, and reckoned I would learn from my mistakes.

The one time I remember being ticked off, and smacked, and then sent to bed, was after a potentially much more serious incident the previous summer.

Neenie pushed back the armchairs and placed a tin bath in the middle of the sitting room in front of the fire. Then she and my mother filled it with steaming kettles and scalding saucepans of water for Sally's bath. She was four. While they returned to the kitchen to heat more water, I chased Sally round and round the room until she tripped into the bath.

I suppose the water wasn't quite hot enough to disfigure her, but she was very badly burned and I remember her howling; I remember my sense of guilt.

When our Norfolk holiday came to an end, there was a ritual. Sally and I went up to see our grandfather in his bedroom where he was waiting for us, propped up by many pillows.

While we thanked him for having us and told him the car was packed, and so on, he arpeggioed his stumpy fingers across his scarlet blanket. Then he drew out from under the blanket a brown ten-shilling note for Sally, this with his left hand, and with his right hand a green one-pound note for me.

Since I was older than Sally, and my parents gave more weekly pocket money to me than to her, I didn't think this was especially unfair. Sally did. I can still see her expression, stoic but pained, the first time that this happened.

But a much more hurtful injustice was the way in which, when I was ten, Neenie invited me to stay at Rahere on my own for an extra week, because I was her 'boy'. This was palpably unfair, and called for my mother, mistress of fair play as she was, to give Sally treats to restore her sense of worth, and balance the books.

For me, though, these were not only favoured but enchanted days in which I basked in my grandmother's love and almost uninterrupted attention. For my grandfather she laid out cold meat, salad, fruit on green dragon plates, all of them covered with muslin in the little pantry, and away we went: by bus to Hunstanton, where we walked the length of the great pier and watched the waves dashing against its legs, and gazed across the Wash and picked out Boston Stump in Lincolnshire; by train from Burnham Market to Wells, and thence to Norwich, where we spent time in Bond's (the department store) and in the market, and always had cream teas in a little restaurant near the cathedral close. Neenie didn't drive, but on some afternoons Grandpa Frank took us out in his grey Hillman Imp, maddeningly never, never exceeding 30 mph, to

Holkham and Brancaster beaches where he read the papers and snoozed while Neenie and I played beach games, and to several churches where I blew the bellows while my grandfather tried out the organ:

> I was the bellows boy. And in corners
> decorated with curious tidemarks
> or up against grey walls frosted with salts
> I pumped and the monsters with twenty throats
> or forty throats shuddered and wheezed.
> Then the old sorcerer showed them his palms
> and soles: they hooted and began to sing.*

As child and as adult, I never once doubted my mother's unconditional love – the steady love given through thick and thin, irrespective of right or wrong. But what Neenie gave me, and my unsentimental, non-physical mother did not, were kisses, hugs, cuddles; necessary, physical comfort.

While I was at Swanbourne, Neenie showered me with letters and food parcels. She often signed her letters, 'with fond love' or 'with fondest love'. Those words precisely describe the tender and wholehearted, uncomplicated way in which she blessed me.

* *Selected Poems*: from 'Generations of Air'.

Uncle Dick and Aunt Rosemary

As a young man, my father was quite foppish and quite self-conscious. He grew his hair long enough for it to curl over his ears, and wore floppy ties. Confronted by my box camera (I still have it), he drapes himself elegantly on lawn or dune and half-closes his eyes, or else looks meaningfully into the mid-distance. In group photos, he is his own man, usually nearest to the camera, with space around him.

When, however, my father was photographed with his younger brother Dick, it was a different matter. He retreated. Now it is handsome, gallant Dick, with his dark hair, piercing blue eyes and irresistible shy smile who stands centre stage, almost athwart the photograph, while my father has reticently taken a step or two backwards. Looking slightly lamed, as if he knows his place, he lowers his eyes.

I have a few snaps of Uncle Dick and my glamorous aunt Rosemary in a nest in the dunes on Scolt Head. Beautifully coiffured, she looks almost as if she has somehow strayed into the sand-and-salt-and-mud of marram-whipped Norfolk from the beach at Cannes.

In actuality, Rosemary was the daughter of Conrad Skinner,

a Methodist minister in Cambridge, renowned not only for coxing the ill-fated Cambridge crew of 1912 (it sank in the Tideway) but for being a faith-healer who made no claims or charges and was possessed of quite remarkable powers.

Once, on our way back from Norfolk, we visited him and his wife in Cambridge. 'No,' he told me. 'I don't touch anyone. There's no need.'

I looked perplexed.

'I lay my hands above the wart or wound or whatever,' he said, 'not on it, and heat passes between us.'

'Where does it come from?' I asked.

'God,' said Conrad Skinner. 'I'm just the conductor.'

My mother admired Aunt Rosemary (I called her that until, in my twenties, she invited me to drop the prefix) for her sharp, analytical intelligence and wit, and so do I. Inevitably, their relationship was slightly rivalrous but, recognising they were both in the same boat with a meek, submissive mother-in-law and an autocratic, self-important father-in-law, they supported each other, and jested about it.

Aunt Rosemary always leavened the proceedings with a certain lightness and brightness, seeing the funny side of things, deflecting the dark.

She told me how, at a village dance in Overy Staithe, she had been pursued by a man she called the Spider, who kept stalking around after her and reaching out towards her, waving his long arms, until my Uncle Dick had shooed him off.

And she told me how she and her elder son Andrew, then aged five, accompanied my grandparents to church – an experience I found increasingly embarrassing as my grandfather always sang twice as loudly as anyone else, and often in harmony. My aunt warned Andrew he would have to keep very quiet and when, immediately outside the church, a car or motorcycle backfired, Andrew whirled round and looked at his mother, appalled.

'I didn't do it!' he protested, while the priest in the sanctuary was saying something about waking and sleeping. 'I didn't wake the Old Man up!'

Once, I perched on my grandfather's leather-seated desk chair at Rahere and watched my aunt knitting.

She dropped a stitch; tried to retrieve it; lost it. 'Well, Kevin!' she said. 'There's nothing for it. Press on regardless!'

This, above all, is what I remember: my aunt's spirited smile and *bon mots*; my uncle's old-world courtesy and inclusiveness:

> You say he'll do right and never great wrong.
> I say he'll always sing the right song
> or stay silent: what I call natural grace.
> You say he will be brave, and face
> all weathers with equanimity.
> I say true teacher; kind and witty.
> You say a man who will love his wife,
> his three children – who will love life!*

Whenever we met, Uncle Dick and Aunt Rosemary seemed to be coming to the end of yet another couple of Gauloises. They lived in wreaths of blue smoke. But what exercises me now is how little we did actually meet – so little that the lives of my three lovely cousins, Andrew, Jonathan and Carolyn (usually known as Honey), who are a little younger than Sally and me, scarcely impinged on me until I was a teenager.

In later years, I saw plainly that my father and Dick, invariably loyal to one another, equally charming and kind and hospitable, maybe equally repressed, lacked an abiding interest in one another's worlds. My father was an artist and intellectual, a philosopher, no family man, antipathetic to sport. My uncle was a fine sportsman and a good sport, he had a 'good war', he was a Francophile, a public-school master and prep-school headmaster, gregarious yet always a family man, and C of E.

But the true wedge was favouritism. Through no fault of his own, Dick was the preferred son, and I suspect that may have

---

* *Selected Poems*: from 'Clay, Syllables, Air'.

bred in my father a slow-burning, deeply concealed resentment that only declared itself much later and then only in part – a resentment and, as the photographs reveal, a sense of inferiority.

Expecting the Best

Never while we were children but now and then in later years my mother spoke affectionately of Bill Waring. Before she met my father, he was her great and, I think, only love, and she became engaged to him when she was eighteen. But after some two years, he broke the engagement off, I don't know why. By all accounts, Bill was a dashing young pilot. He flew wartime missions to Norway, and, when his own marriage broke up in 1950 or 1951, he contacted my mother again in the hope of reawakening their romance. With her own husband faithless and her marriage arid, my mother agreed to see Bill again, only to have second thoughts and pull out on the very day they were to meet.

Sometimes I think of my father as a sensual seeker, a man whose strong spiritual, artistic and intellectual leanings were attended by a delight in bodily pleasures, and of my mother as a chaste sensualist, a woman alive to her own bloom, fitness and health, more practical than intellectual, conditioned by imposed and self-imposed physical restraint and separacy. Increasingly, she had to find channels other than her marriage through which to express her passionate nature.

Most parents say they want the best for their children; not so many have a precise idea of what that best is, and are prepared to make sacrifices to achieve it.

Perhaps my mother believed her marriage could somehow weather the storm of my father's intense and sustained affair. At all events, she decided that it was in Sally's and my best interests to stay within it. To stay within it not for a month or for a year and to see how things went; rather to stay within her marriage for better, for worse, for richer, for poorer – if not until death . . .

'I decided to stay with Daddy until you were both grown-up,' my mother told me. 'He thought it was best too.'

Those words beg so many questions. Did my mother decide and my father tag along? Did they ever once really discuss it? My father was so good at sticking his head in the sand and avoiding or, anyhow, skirting round emotional needs and truths. Did the fact that my mother owned Crosskeys (given to her by her father) have any bearing on my father's thinking? Did he do more than pay lip-service to their decision? And how far was it influenced by their circle of Chiltern friends in which, so far as I can remember, there was not a single separation or divorce? One can assert that my parents' choice was a child of its own time, but one cannot really say that it was right or wrong.

Never one to do things by halves, my mother threw herself with enormous gusto into our upbringing.

Because she believed that private schools offered the best education, she went to great lengths to ensure that I received it, and in later years often unjustly criticised herself because Sally, then at the Rambert Ballet School, 'never had the same chance as you'.

My mother's aim was to show us excellence of all kinds, the discipline and delight of serious play, and the splendour of Britain on display.

She took us to the Festival of Britain and the Royal Tournament at Olympia; she took us to an open-topped

Jaguar race at Silverstone – I have a snap of the start; she took us to a pageant at Saint Albans and to meets of the Old Berkeley Hunt (West) at Little Kimble and Owlswick; she drove us down to the Badminton Horse Trials where, with my Brownie, I took a close-up photo of the new queen.

I write she . . . she . . . Did my father not come to any of these events? Some of them, maybe, though he had no interest whatsoever in sport. My father engaged with us in matters of the mind and imagination, but in most other respects my mother made the running.

When I was ten, the children of Whiteleaf played a home cricket match against Stokenchurch. Kitted and padded, and with such high hopes, I ploughed out to bat on the strip where I'd so often watched my heroes – especially Dr Cooper, who hit one six into the adjacent golf course – setting about their opponents.

I survived two balls and was clean bowled by the third. Chastened, I retreated to the boundary and to my mother. For her, action was a far better palliative than undue sympathy and the next day she wrote to her father's brother, Somerset (always known as Uncle Sommie), a member of the MCC, to ask him whether he could arrange for me to be coached at Lord's!

Not only that. That same summer, my mother took me to Lord's to see the test match between England and South Africa. I watched, more than that, I *lived* a stand between Compton and Edrich – and later, in my bedroom, replayed just about every stroke; I gazed at the sward, with its almost mesmerising cross-mown strips of green; I clapped with great zest; and I caught my breath when, all around me, the crowd suddenly bellowed.

Never much of a cricketer, this boy started to follow all the county scores and all the individual scores and bowling figures, day by day, and did so for season after season. And when, now a grey-haired man, he was ushered on a test match morning into the ECB's box at Lord's, and greeted by David Morgan, he thought he had entered Eden . . .

In this way and many, my resourceful mother turned setback to advantage. She expected the best and expected I would never give less than my best; I tried to oblige.

The King is Dead. Long Live the Queen!

School assembly on my eleventh birthday, 7 February 1952, did not follow its usual course. Instead of striding into the double classroom where we were all awaiting him, and beginning by congratulating any birthday boys, Mr Evans stood at the door and announced, 'Fast falls the eventide. We'll begin today with Hymn 331.' At once Miss Noakes struck up the doleful tune and, conservative as children are, we were all rather apprehensive as we sang:

> Where is death's sting? Where, grave, thy victory? . . .
> Heaven's morning breaks, and earth's vain shadows flee;
> In life, in death, O Lord, abide with me!

As soon as the hymn had ended, the headmaster advanced quietly through the ranks.

'I've very sad news for you this morning,' he said. 'Our king has died.'

I remember thinking at once that I didn't feel sad about this, because I didn't really know anything much about the king, but that I could see it made Mr Evans and the other staff sad. And then I wondered whether my parents knew and whether they felt sad too.

I wasn't brought up in a bubble but, with no daily newspaper and no television at home or school, our knowledge of national and world events was almost wholly contingent on what our teachers and parents chose to tell and discuss with us.

Mr Evans then gave us a cameo portrait of King George VI, a gentle, hesitant, dutiful man. He told us about his wife and two daughters.

'He had a good innings,' Mr Evans concluded, his voice brightening. 'Yes, a good innings.'

This was language we all understood. We all knew life was not only an individual but a team game, and the elect amongst us had been awarded a new cricket ball for scoring fifty or, the supreme accolade, a new bat for scoring a century for the First XI against another school. We understood that, being born of a woman, we must all in the end necessarily die, and that while the king's death was momentous and deeply regrettable it was not untimely. In point of fact, this was by no means wholly true. King George VI had been dogged by ill health all his life, undergone a serious operation for lung disease the previous September, and was only fifty-seven when he died.

At break, I fetched my portable radio and propped it on a large radiator, the kind that shudders and bellows and groans; I tuned it in to the Home Service, and a whole group of us crowded around it.

But it told us nothing about the king. Instead, we all found ourselves in the middle of a programme about the history and achievement of the football club Tottenham Hotspur.

I was fascinated and, after my friends had drifted away, climbed back to my dormitory with my hot-bottomed transistor pressed to my ear.

Tottenham Hotspur . . . not royal association nor meaning but sheer sound, the balance and energy of those words held me in thrall. Tottenham Hotspur! There and then, I became an ardent fan, and I've followed the team's fortunes ever since.

During the summer term of the following year, 1953, we were all given a whole week's holiday to celebrate the coronation, and watched long hours of it, frame by black-and-white frame, in the crowded sitting room of Sally's and my piano teacher, Mrs Carwithen, one of our few friends to have television. And then, in the June dusk, as the drizzle died away and the skies cleared over the Chilterns, almost every able-bodied man, woman and child living in the village picked and puffed their way to the top of the hill.

A little way along the ridge from the Cross stood the most enormous bonfire, still unlit, awaiting the dark.

Remembering it now, I'm conscious how through the centuries we have used fires on hills and headlands to celebrate, to mourn and to warn. When the great hero Beowulf (in the Anglo-Saxon poem of that name) dies, poisoned by the dragon's venom, his followers drag up wood to Whaleness and build a great pyre high on the headland. And when the Armada was sighted in 1588, hillfires were lit the length and breadth of England. This, too, is what happened on the night of the coronation:

> The huge bonfire blazed. Its heart was brighter and darker than anything I've ever seen, and it spat golden and orange fireflies at the stars. All around us, white faces and black faces gambolled and gallumphed and gallivanted and shouted and sang.[*]

On Bledlow Rise and Chinnor Hill and all over the Vale of Aylesbury we could see burning beacons, nine in all, the nearest cream-orange and flickering, the furthest as far off as the freezing stars.

My parents and their friends seemed as joyous as we were, somehow let off the hook of the humdrum. For their generation, the gift of the coronation was new energy, new hope.

Later that summer term, the whole school was taken on an

* From *The Seeing Stone*.

outing to Aylesbury. There we went to the Odeon to see a double bill. The first thirty-minute film showed Sir John Hunt's expedition to Everest, culminating in the ascent by Sir Edmund Hillary and Tenzing while the second, *The Queen is Crowned*, was an edited full-colour version of the coronation.

My mother reminded me to be sure to watch out for the splendid Queen of Tonga who, alone amongst the host of royals and other dignitaries, braved the drizzle and rode in an open carriage to Westminster Abbey, thereby winning the British public's lasting affection.

During the first few months after the coronation, the young queen made a number of progresses through London and other big cities to show herself to her people: acts of dedication, revelation and celebration. (My mother seldom missed an opportunity such as this – as much on her own account as on ours – and I remember how crestfallen she was when, in my mid-teens, I declined to go with her to hear Churchill give his last electioneering speech in Woodford.) She and Sally and I duly took the train up to London and then went by underground to Saint Paul's. I was shocked by the way in which so many buildings around the cathedral had been flattened by bombs, and there were still so many piles of rubble.

This, of course, was part of my mother's plan and a cue to talk about the Blitz, the King and Queen's bravery in staying put in Buckingham Palace, the virtues of our new young Queen . . .

For hours, my mother, Sally and I stood on one of the bleachers lining the roadside somewhere near Saint Paul's. As on the top of Whiteleaf Cross, strangers talked like friends, and class counted for nothing.

The Queen wore her crown.

Ritual is like glue: then and even now bonding society, stabilising it.

King Arthur

Whiteleaf Cross! On the ridge a bonfire licked and cracked, signalling the coronation of the new young Queen; while somewhere within it, in a chill stone chamber, biding his time, lay the Welsh king . . .

It was five years since my father had told me (when I was six) about sleeping Arthur and, though I could not prove it and realised it was unlikely – what, after all, was the king doing in the Chiltern Hills when his battles were fought in the west and south-west? – I still did not discount it.

Often, my father excited my imagination with talk of Mons Badonicus, site of Arthur's great victory over the Anglo-Saxons, and of Merlin and the Round Table and, more interested in ideal and quest than in historicity, he remained fascinated by the Arthurian legends all his life.

He often asked me whether I could find my way into Camelot. That eventually I tried to do so was in no small part due to him, and I'm glad he had read the first part of my Arthur trilogy, *The Seeing Stone*, before his sudden death.

My father flagged one short passage in that book that especially struck him. In his stone, the squire Arthur de Caldicot sees and hears Sir Pellinore asserting, 'Each of us must have a dream to light our way through this dark world,' in reply to the mysterious hooded man's affirmation that 'Each of us needs a quest, and a person without one is lost to himself.'

My father opened his eyes and looked at me and his eyes glimmered. 'That is a *very* serious thing to say,' he murmured, and then he closed his eyes again.

Many of the songs my father composed when I was a boy are about states of in-between – desire, dream and twilight – while his tone-poem for pianoforte, *The Distant Isle*, a response to the old Irish poem about Bran's voyage, might as well be about Avalon.

I do remember listening with my father to Bax's orchestral tone poem, *Tintagel*, but what's surprising is that I didn't comb the library for children's versions of Arthurian legend, and that my father did not introduce me to passages of Malory or Tennyson, or show me medieval or Pre-Raphaelite paintings. As it was, I had to content myself with so many rereadings of H. E. Marshall's two exceedingly brief chapters about King Arthur that I virtually knew them by heart.

During the 1930s my father had visited Tintagel and come back with a hoard of forty postcards. A few of these portray and describe items central to Arthurian legend, such as 'The Sangreal' and 'The Sword Excalibur' and 'The Lance', a few describe the trappings of knighthood ('The Golden Spur', 'The Sword of a Knight', 'Emblem of the Knights of the Round Table'), but most are devoted to the coats-of-arms of the Knights of the Round Table.

When I was eleven, my father presented these cards to me for the museum, and for hours I stared at Sir Tristram's harp and the two hearts, those of Tristram and Isolde, each transfixed by two arrows; the Saracen knight Sir Palomides's five white stars on a black background; Sir Ironside's three interlocking silver rings; Sir Mordred's shield, wholly black; and Sir Persides de Bloise's verdant shield with its splendid ramping gold lion with a scarlet tongue.

I pored over the succinct, high-falutin' but provocative texts below each coat-of-arms. Of Sir Persides, I read:

> Sir Persides, son of Sir Pellounes, was a Knight of the Round Table but he lived in his own castle and went on adventure alone. He sought lodging one night at a castle near a stone bridge, and because it was against his honour as a knight to yield to the evil custom of the lady of the castle, he was chained to a post on the bridge . . .

Sir Mordred was 'a spy, betrayer, informer and violator of any trust reposed in him'; Sir Pertolepe wore green armour; Sir Breunor slew a lion that endangered Queen Guinevere's life. Of King Mark, I learned, 'no good can be said . . . for he was a coward and a murderer'. Sir Kay had 'a cruel habit of nicknaming young knights', while at every tournament Sir Dagonet 'made King Arthur laugh, and for his good nature and cheerfulness he was very popular at Court'.

Here, and not between the covers of any book, I really got my first taste of the passion, intrigue and values of the Arthurian legends, and I was utterly hooked.

On the reverse side of each postcard were the words 'THE ADDRESS ONLY TO BE WRITTEN HERE' and 'A Souvenir from King Arthur's Hall at Tintagel' and 'CORRESPONDENCE FOR INLAND POSTAGE ONLY'.

I shuffled my Camelot pack and wondered who, owning such priceless treasure, could bear to part with even one fortieth of it.

Massacre

Home for the summer holidays, I treated Sally as the imperious captain of the First XI might treat his youngest, most eager apprentice. I expected obedience. I expected admiration. And in return, the best Sally could expect from me was a brother's terse approval.

'Sally, you've got to – you've got to score seven runs – you've got to get your left leg across – you've got to catch it.'

On dry days, I set up the stumps in our little garden; and if not the stumps, then the canvas archery target with its straw padding, or else I got out the Jokari bats, and Sally had to endure the small, hard rubber ball whizzing around her ears. On wet days, we pursued this unequal competition indoors. We played marbles, board games and, above all, interminable games of OWZAT, during which I religiously kept the score, ball by ball and run by run.

But then the holidays were punctuated – more than that, they were punctured – by three events, each more upsetting than the previous one.

The first was that my sister somehow contrived to swallow a kirby grip. This was the signal for our mother to serve up meal after meal of porridge, mixing into Sally's steaming bowl wisps and shreds of cotton wool. Sally wasn't allowed to take any physical exercise; she wasn't even allowed outdoors. She was cocooned outside and in, and my mother told me that if I upset her, she would never forgive me. I imagined the grip grabbing hold of Sally's guts, or piercing the wall of her stomach, and stayed quiet.

This Red Alert lasted for two or three days. Then the kirby grip reappeared, wrapped in cotton wool, and Sally was allowed out to play again.

The second event was that our ginger cat ate Sally's budgerigar.

The loss of a pet is often a child's first direct experience of death, both shocking and very painful. But what Sally remembers is the way in which, as so often, our relentless mother also saw and pounced on an opportunity. That same evening, she asked Sally to feed the cat. When Sally demurred, understandably enough, my mother insisted.

'This is how things are,' she told her. 'Death in life. Life in death.'

But it was the third event that really bonded brother and sister. Bright-eyed, ears pricked, intelligent to a fault, Bruce once again broke all the rules, burst into a local hen-coop, and massacred the inmates – all of them.

This was one atrocity too many, and a number of our neighbours complained to my parents that Bruce was a menace, a killer, and they were afraid he might even attack people.

'Never!' Sally protested to my mother. 'Not unless they was molesting your children!'

This attempt to view the situation from my mother's viewpoint, and to arouse her protective instinct, much appealed to my mother, as did Sally's use of the same rhetorical device after getting back to Crosskeys from school and finding no one there.

'You should be here waiting,' Sally complained as soon as our mother turned up, 'when your childrens get home from school.'

Be that as it may, Bruce's fate was sealed, and no amount of protests or appeals could have saved him.

Early one morning, Sally and I were packed off to spend the whole day with family friends, and when we got back, Bruce was not there.

Our mother and father sat us down in the sitting room – regrettably, we called it the lounge.

They told us very seriously that, as Bruce had got into such trouble, they had decided to send him away to a new home on the other side of the country, in Wiltshire.

We believed them.

We understood, and wept, and accepted that it had to be. So trusting, so unsuspecting, we even swallowed our parents' explanation that they hadn't told us in advance because we would have been even more upset. And when, a couple of years later, my mother drove us down to Wiltshire to see our old nurse May and her demon husband Frank, we begged her to let us visit Bruce in his new home, so that we could see him once more.

Unlike my father, my mother never shied away from emotional confrontation, but she also never inflicted on her children more than they needed or were ready to know.

Only years later did Sally and I learn that, while we had been playing with our friends on the other side of the village, our beloved Bruce had – to use one of the beastly euphemisms associated with death – been put down.

French Exchanges

When my parents didn't want Sally or me to understand what they were saying, they spoke in French. This was so frustrating that I used to try to interrupt them by hopping round and round the kitchen table on my left leg, or lifting myself bodily on the front rail of the Aga. So I was excited to hear that a boy from Luxembourg was coming to stay for two weeks during the summer holidays so I could learn better French and he could learn better English, even when my mother told me that I would have to share my room with him and that the national dish in Luxembourg was lark pie.

Johnmari, a curious hybrid of a name, arrived midway through the holidays before I went to Swanbourne in 1951, and he was succeeded by Jean-Pierre and Laurent during the following summers.

While the principle behind these exchanges was of course a good one, the practice was rather a shock. It meant that I had a rival on my own doorstep, inseparable as a shadow, whom I had to treat with courtesy because he was my guest. It meant that for most of the time I was supposed to correct his English. Sally, moreover, very young as she was and much as she may deny it now, was not impervious to Gallic charm, and that piqued me.

What strikes me, looking at the images of Johnmari and Jean-Pierre and Laurent that grace my mother's photo albums, is how un-English they are: charming, yes, and half-smiling, slightly supercilious, somehow inward, well-dressed, well-groomed.

Johnmari was ready to try his hand at cricket; and Jean-Pierre and I rubbed along well enough. But although Laurent helped me to polish the wondrous shield given to me by my grandfather, things were altogether different. We began to argue, and our arguments soon got worse, exacerbated by the fact that he spoke poor English and I spoke worse French, so neither of us could say what we really meant.

These annual exchanges were naturally meant to introduce us to cultural difference, and to something of one another's history; and so when we took Laurent with us to Norfolk, where Grandpa Frank spoke fluent French, we showed him Nelson's birthplace – just a plaque on a wall in the village of Burnham Thorpe, facing the limpid, tautologous stream known as the Burn. And then I led Laurent round a hedge to the ship-shaped pond that Horatio had dug out as a boy.

This was like a red rag to a bull, and by the time we stepped into Burnham Thorpe church, stashed with Nelsoniana and draped with white ensigns, we were arguing furiously if incoherently about all the virtues and defects of Nelson and Napoleon.

The bad feeling between us would not go away; partly, I suppose, because we were unable to express it, partly because I was playing at home and Laurent away. Back in Whiteleaf the argument erupted again. When my mother had to go over to Aylesbury with Sally for the afternoon, she arranged for Laurent and me to visit friends in the village, but Laurent refused to come with me.

When I got home, there was nobody there. My mother and Sally hadn't come back, and Laurent had disappeared.

I was rather scared and remember waiting anxiously in the garage. My mother took a quick look round my room and immediately bundled Sally and me into the car.

We picked up Laurent on the main road between Monks Risborough and Princes Risborough, a forlorn figure in very short shorts, carrying a heavy brown suitcase.

He told my mother he was unhappy. He told her he'd decided to go home, and was on his way to Princes Risborough station – not that he had any tickets or more than a few coins.

'No,' my mother told me that evening, 'he wouldn't have got very far, but that's not the point, and you know it's not.'

Relieved, resentful, chastened, tearful, yes, Laurent and I were all those things. And this was, I think, the moment at which Gisèle, one of the Findlays' French governesses, was brought into play, and offered Laurent the *soutienne morale* that, with my own newfound caution, made the remainder of his visit bearable.

When I was sixteen and Sally thirteen, we went to stay with tetchy Laurent and his rather appealing sister Pascale for three whole weeks – one in Paris, one near Lurcy-Levy in the Auvergne, and one near Chamonix in the Alps – with a view to substantially improving our French. My letters home declare Laurent's manners to be as bad as his mother's, and note that Pascale is 'quite objectionable and always arguing with someone' and 'takes offence far too easily', while my diary makes several mentions of Laurent's and my continuing 'rows' and 'blow-outs'. On our very last day, Laurent's mother, Madame Gruson, left us at Les Invalides, saying with a gay smile that she'd collect us a couple of hours later as she wanted us to have 'ample time' to admire Napoleon's tomb.

This was no more than I deserved, but I still bridled at it, not least because Sally was caught up in the crossfire. But loyal as ever, my sister was indignant on my behalf and just as uncomfortable at all the reverence and emotion swilling around the appallingly grandiose monument as she had been when Naomi wept buckets of tears at *Carmen*. She made her own effective intervention at supper that last evening.

I was just looking across the table at plain-but-pretty Pascale, rueing how little romantic headway I'd made with her, when Madame Gruson placed in front of each of us a tournedos. A big treat, she said, because it was our last dinner in France. Then Monsieur Gruson poured us glasses of red wine.

Madame Gruson looked around the table in satisfaction while her family tucked their white linen napkins over their collars and all began to eat at breakneck speed.

When I cut my steak, blood oozed from it. The round of meat was soft, almost bouncy. My gravy turned red.

'Sally!' I said helplessly.

Sally grasped the situation at once. She picked up her glass of red wine and poured half of it over my tournedos.

'This is what we do in England!' she announced blithely. And then she turned to me. 'Now eat it!' she ordered me under her breath.

Black Waxworks

'You must remain kneeling,' says R. S. Thomas in his wonderful poem 'The Moon in Lleyn', and that's what I did: first rubbing church brasses; and later, throughout much of my teens, as an ordinand.

One winter morning when I was eleven, I went scavenging in the churchyard of Saint Dunstan's at Monks Risborough, kicking over molehills in the hope of finding pieces of sturdy medieval green glaze and brown glaze to bring back to the museum. It was so cold the tops of the molehills were icy and frosted.

When I wandered round the light, spacious church, I saw the brass of one of its mid-fifteenth-century rectors, Robert Blundell. He was slim, his fingers tapered, he had a large forehead and was well-coiffured, the collar and sleeves and hem of his vestments were embroidered with little crosses as pretty as Alpine wildflowers. For a long time I looked down at him, and then in the chancel I knelt beside him. Unaware that this elegant, dully gleaming figure in no way represented the way Robert Blundell actually looked, I felt I half-knew him, this man who somehow resembled my father, and whose six church bells I could hear tolling, tolling when I was sitting on the top of Whiteleaf Cross and the wind was blowing from the past to the present.

'You could rub the brass,' my mother said.

'What do you mean?'

'I'll find out what materials you need.'

In about 1960, brass-rubbing became fashionable in England. Some churches charged rubbing fees; a few deconsecrated churches opened as brass-rubbing centres. But my interest in church-brasses preceded all this.

Equipped by my mother with rolls of white drawer-lining paper and sticks of hard black wax, I used to cycle alone from church to church in the neighbourhood, searching for brasses to rub.

More often than not, I arrived centuries too late, and found nothing but a matrix and, maybe, a brass pin or two; I learned about palimpsests, and felt sorry for the individuals whose identity had in some way been pilfered or compromised; I stared up at brasses affixed to damp walls, impossible to rub because there was no satisfactory way of hanging or securing paper over them.

Before long, my mother began to take a much more active interest in my brass-rubbing. She ferried me to churches all over Buckinghamshire, she stretched and held down the paper so that I achieved far better impresses than my first paltry attempts, she reminded me to make a careful record of who and when and where, and she encouraged me to experiment, providing me with softer honey-coloured wax and, back at home, bottles of black ink.

True enough, the ink ran off the waxed paper and picked out the incisions – the facial features and folds in the clothing and the like – but it also drew attention to all the little pits and pocks the brass had collected through the generations. I reverted to black wax.

Sally has told me how, as a girl, she sometimes put out hesitant tendrils only for my mother to swamp her interest in learning or doing something new.

'First she egged me on, but then she got in my way,' Sally says. 'Her great eagerness intimidated me. It made me less confident.'

How precious confidence is. For my part, I knew that my enterprise pleased my mother; and I welcomed, even required, her growing involvement in it. But what I did not see then was how lonely she was. So I suppose our expeditions also offered her a kind of companionship and creative partnership.

When I was twelve and had visited most of the brasses in the county, and rubbed a good number of them, I decided it was time to compile a guidebook to them. So, after the music and passion of *I LOVE THE WATRIS* and the ambition and event of *The History of the World/History of the British Isles*, this was my third literary undertaking, by design more informative than imaginative, *Church Brasses in Buckinghamshire*.

For her part, my mother explored the possibility of reproducing some of our rubbings as Christmas cards, and marketing them. The printer's first attempt lacked body and looked rather scuffed and scratched, but the reproductions of Sir Robert Ingylton and his wife, who both died in 1472 and whose brasses lie side by side in Thornton parish church, were strikingly beautiful: the gold foil looked brassy, the black ink was matt and dense.

Through the good offices of a mutual friend, Gordon Fraser offered to undertake international distribution of our cards, draft contracts were prepared, and a round table conference proposed. This fell through, I don't know why, but my mother then secured an immediate small order from Heal's and the possibility of a very much larger order from Harrods for the following year. But nothing came of this either because, during the next twelve months, reproductions of brass-rubbings suddenly began to appear all over the place.

Just now and then, as a result of intuition, application or sheer good luck, we may find ourselves in a position where we're a half-step ahead of everyone else, and when this happens, we must try to take full advantage of it at once. My mother rued that she had not driven a hard enough bargain, and was never in any doubt that she had only very narrowly missed a chance of making us both some money.

My parents were already in the habit of sending handmade or specially printed Christmas cards and that year, 1952, they sent Sir Robert Ingylton or his wife to family and friends. In return, the weaver Theo Moorman sent a little snitch of glittering threads, mounted on cream card; and as was their wont for many years, Bruno and Rita Bronowski sent a combined effort, her illustration and his poem.

For some years, I kept a store of my brass-rubbing cards for special people and special occasions, and in 1960 I sent one as a Christmas card to R. S. Thomas after paying him a pilgrimage at Eglwys Fach near Machynlleth. Given his courteous but astringent reservations about my first stumbling poems, I dare say he was quite glad to be able to offer it unconditional praise.

Bat-droppings, their acid eating into the brass; the damp corners of church walls frosted with salts; aching forearms and shoulders and necks, aching knees.

How I loved all this. My little guidebook is simple and straightforward but leavened with a map and drawings, littered with adjectives – 'unusual', 'tragic', 'amusing', 'amazing' – and punctuated with brief digressions describing churches innocent of brasses, such as Saint Bartholomew's at Fingest, with its strange saddleback tower, that I had visited on bicycle rides. Reading it again now, I rediscover facts I'd forgotten I once knew: 'A brass was made out of 60 per cent copper, 30 per cent zinc, and 5 per cent each of lead and tin, although the latter two are often found in even smaller quantities. The metal was imported from Germany and the Low Countries and often from Cologne whence comes the name *Cullen* plate.'

The Great Flood of 1953

During my first year at Swanbourne, I slept in a convivial, noisy dormitory with nine other boys. But returning in September 1952 for my second year, I found I was in a much smaller room, and just one of three inmates: the dormitory captain – I'll call him Licker Lonsdale – and Murdin, and me. Here, it was infinitely less companionable, and very much more exposed.

During half-term, my mother took Sally and me to *Annie, Get Your Gun* at the Playhouse in Oxford, and when I told Murdin and the dormitory captain about this, Licker Lonsdale's eyes lightened. He got out of bed, put on his outdoor shoes, and began to tap dance and sing.

I was hugely impressed, and it wasn't long before he offered to teach me:

> Licker Lonsdale could tap dance.
> His hot eyes stripped us
> naked so Murdin the Mole used to burrow
> beneath his blankets before
> lights out.*

* From *Selected Poems*: 'Preparatory School'.

I paid for my lessons beneath Licker Lonsdale's blankets. For a few minutes, he fondled my genitals, I fondled his, and then I hopped back into my own bed again.

I neither welcomed nor resisted this occasional practice. What scared me was having to rely on Murdin's discretion, and the thought that other boys would find out about it. If I close my eyes, I can visualise that dormitory: its one large eye and shapeless curtains, the cream walls, the light-fitting on its long chain, the position of Murdin's and Licker Lonsdale's beds. The one thing I cannot see is my own bed: as if I were denying I really lived in that space and that body because I was so heavily dependent and, I suppose, uncertain of myself.

At the beginning of the spring term, the dormitory captain's attentions and requirements became rather more pressing, and so it was something of a relief as well as a complete surprise when, on Sunday 1 February, Harold Evans told me to get packed because my mother was on her way over to collect me.

'She and your father are driving up to Norfolk,' he said. 'To look after your grandparents and see the storm damage.'

Armed with permission to miss Monday's and Tuesday's classes and games, and with that sense of elation unexpected freedom gives, I sat next to Sally in the back of the car, with not the least idea of what awaited us.

It was already dark when we arrived. Sally and I bundled up and ran down to the creek and at once we stumbled into great mounds of flotsam and jetsam and weed next to the Maltings, but we had no idea of the devastation all around us. It was only early next morning that we saw how our summer playground had been changed into a winter war zone.

That evening, on my grandparents' crackling radio, we heard how the whole of the east coast had taken a terrible beating when powerful northerly gales produced a storm surge in the North Sea – a surge that coincided with a spring tide on the evening of Saturday 31 January.

We listened to the litany of loss, and the stunning statistics: 307

people drowned; the coastline breached in more than one thousand places; twenty-four thousand homes flooded; one hundred and sixty thousand acres of farmland overwhelmed; forty-six thousand livestock drowned. The moving slate memorial in Hunstanton is witness to the loss of whole families of United States servicemen, Bailey and Richardson and Branch and Martin.

Sally and I hurried down to the creek again before breakfast, and almost at once rushed back to Rahere, and woke up our parents.

'You've got to get up,' I told them. 'You've got to!'

Then we reported to Neenie what we'd seen. 'Mounds of debris all over the Bells' tennis court . . . The water's smashed down the big doors of the Maltings . . . The Sharpies are all higgledy-piggledy, some of them are upside down . . . There's a huge blue boat stranded in East Harbour Way, you know, outside the doctor's house. She's lying on her keel . . . You can't even drive down to the Staithe.'

With our parents we began to pick our way along muddy Burnham Dyke. The sea-giant had lifted the huge hunks of concrete lining the bank and hurled them all over the place – into the oozing muddy creek, on to the top of the dyke, and right over it. Then we came to where there was no going beyond: Burnham Dyke (some say Bank) is maybe twelve foot high and at least twice as broad at its base, but the pounding waves had punched a hole in it thirty or forty yards long and inundated the freshwater marshes on the other side of it. I could scarcely believe my eyes.

Later that day, we drove some way east along the coast. Marvellously, the north wall of Holkham Hall estate remained in one piece, something I wrote about in an early poem, trying to echo the pounding music of Anglo-Saxon poetry:

Relentless, the sea rolls down from the Pole.
It levelled the dunes last year, removed the marram grass,
clashed its steel cymbals over marsh and macadam.
It attacked me and undermined me: I sway

like a drunkard now; yet it could not gash me
with its gleaming scythes; it was not strong enough.
I stand, sad, and stare at all this estate,
the lawns, the kitchen gardens, copses garrulous
in the wind. I carefully listen, listen and wait
for the fierce outsider to force his way in.*

At Holkham, a bull tethered outside the wall had just been
able to keep his head above water. But in Wells-next-the-Sea,
there was a 160-ton MTB beached on the quay, looking
quite monstrous, and all the fishing-boats were herded
against the sea-wall after dragging their moorings.
Salthouse, bleak enough at the best of times, was a wrecked,
abandoned hamlet in the middle of a wasteland of debris,
seaweed and stones.

Bit by bit, Sally's and my early excitement, intoxication
almost, gave way to a mood far more sombre. The extent of
the devastation was overwhelming, and while my father
inclined to let it speak for itself, my mother kept impressing on
us the cost in human terms.

In Overy Staithe, Mrs Riches's Post Office shop was jammed
with people exchanging news:

> And that once, horrified,
> leaning right across her counter:

> 'Foive at Heacham
> and Wilkie's boat wedged
> up East Harbour Way
> and that owd MTB
> dumped on the quay at Wells
> and sin the sandbags
> and first owd Arthur knew was water
> through his keyhole . . .'

> No tale, not even this,

---

* *Selected Poems*: from 'The Wall'.

quite all told
in this spiced corner of paradise,
the bell always being rung.*

No one respects the sea like those who live close by it and depend on it for their livelihood, and it didn't take the East Coast floods for people to recognise that England is, as it were, on a tilt, and that year by year, yard by yard, the land is losing its battle with the sea. Money poured into coastal defences and 'managing the environment' can delay the inevitable but, as climate change quickens, the mood is distinctly wary and apprehensive.

Listening to eyewitness accounts at once terrifying and inspiring as paradigms of courage and survival, reading how the rubber-suited US airman Reis Leming single-handedly saved the lives of twenty-seven people in Hunstanton, looking at the flood-level plaque attached to the water mill in Burnham Overy Staithe and seeing how water rushed up the course of the Burn and imprisoned people in their bedrooms; hearing how the tide swept through the ground floor of the Phillips's Moorings Hotel; staring out at imperilled Marsh Farm at Burnham Norton, the setting for my children's books, *Storm* and *Waterslain Angels*; surrounded by knowledgeable talk about sea levels rising and the increasing likelihood of storm surges, one's only too well aware that it's no longer a question of whether but where and when.

Although we remained in Norfolk only for one full day and a couple of nights, the impact of what we had seen was massive and long lasting. I am still working it out in my poems, in which the ocean may be appealing, magnetic even, but is seldom gentle, often treacherous or wild, always shape-changing.

In North Norfolk there is plenty of squelch but little that is mellow or nesh. The landscape speaks of survival and the beauty, sometimes subtle, sometimes simple, of the hard-won. I suppose these are the qualities I aspire to in my poems.

* *Selected Poems*: from 'Waterslain: Mrs Riches'.

When my parents and Sally deposited me at Swanbourne in time for high tea on Tuesday, I felt as if I'd been away for a very long time. I felt drained too, and quite glad to be back 'where all's accustomed, ceremonious', even if rather too exposed. I lugged my brown suitcase up to my little Cyclopean dormitory.

Coaching at Lord's

My mother's letter to her Uncle Sommie, written after my poor showing in the cricket match against Stokenchurch, bore fruit.

On 18 March 1953, he forwarded me a card from the MCC specifying the dates of my coaching. And ten days later he wrote to my mother:

> First of all as regards Kevin he should take white shorts, shirt, pullover and white cricket boots, but I think you will find they have to be rubber not spiked as they will be playing on matting, but if you have any doubt perhaps you could get Peter to ring up the Secretary.

I imagine my mother snorted at this suggestion. Before they were married, she had taken my father on his one and only visit to Lord's, and he sat with his back to the game for most of the time because he was notating a new song and the sun got in his eyes.

In fact, my father's complete lack of interest in sport had long made me despair. He had no plimsolls and, when he finally agreed to a game of tennis, he played against me on a hard court with bare feet. And once, when I came back from

Brancaster beach, mightily impressed that I had not only met but bowled at a member of the Lincolnshire 2nd XI, with the county badge on his sleeveless sweater, he simply smiled and closed his eyes.

So of course it was my mother who rang up the Secretary of the MCC, and she who proudly escorted me, properly kitted out and nicely groomed, through the North Gate at Lord's.

I recall how my mother also drove me over to Wimbledon when I was eighteen and playing in the Youll Cup. I'd decided to grow a beard only a few days before and, to her disgust, refused to shave. She and Sally sat in the front, and I remember she kept looking at me in the rearview mirror and saying how awful I looked.

The coaching at Lord's lasted for four or five days. The pupils were all much my age, elevens and twelves and thirteens, and the staff were professionals, some of them old internationals, including Laurie Fishlock, who had been a Wisden Cricketer of the Year only six years before.

In the spacious Nursery, the open nets, and the nets set up in the echoing arcades, we batted, bowled offspin, tried to bowl leg-spin, bowled at pace, used the cradle, learned to throw flat and hard. During the breaks, we talked about Sheppard and Laker and Trueman and May.

'I am very pleased,' Uncle Sommie wrote to my mother, 'to hear Kevin . . . so thoroughly enjoyed it. Will you please thank him very much for his letter and tell him I look forward to great things in the cricket world this next term?'

Great things? No. Not then nor afterwards. I was more eager than able, though apparently a reasonably stylish batsman.

But from that April on, I started to keep my own scoring-book when I listened to test matches on the radio; at Swanbourne, I volunteered to help roll the dewy 1st XI pitch with the heavy Ironcrete, before haring back up to the school for breakfast; I oiled my bat and dreamed linseed-and-willow dreams . . .

I see myself standing alone in Swanbourne's cricket pavilion, in actuality a small corrugated-iron shed no bigger than my museum. Around me are old pads, gloves backed with chewed green rubber spikes, a broken bat, other paraphernalia. I'm alone there, looking out across the bright green pitch through the small covered opening, and it's raining, gently raining.

I don't know why I was there alone, or exactly when. What I remember is a sense of warmth and lack of impatience. Somewhere, maybe, between preparation and action, dream and waking, I sensed how cricket includes many dressing-rooms, rehearsals, hopes, fears. A subtle and beautiful, serious and play-ful game that unfolds on the field and in the head and the heart.

Scout Camp

The words Kevin and Scout do not rhyme. They do not even strike a spark like flint clashed against steel.

I've only to voice the word 'scout' or 'guide' and my wife Linda and Dick, my brother-in-law, will straighten their backs. Their eyes will brighten. They were both patrol leaders. For me, scouting signified inadequacy, erosion of confidence, and fear.

During term time at Swanbourne, the scout troop met once each week; and while this seemed a complete waste of a perfectly good sporting afternoon, it was at least manageable. I've managed to suppress most of the unpleasant memories of what we actually did, but we certainly spent a good deal of time scuffling around in always-damp Scout Wood (you were only allowed to enter it if you were a scout), snapping twigs, making smoky fires and lumpy porridge, pancakes, twists, dampers and even mutton, onion and potato stew. When it was raining, we retreated to the scout loft and learned to map-read, and practised tying knots I still can't tie. My 'Song of the Knots', written for children a couple of years ago, was simply an expiation:

(to be read rhythmically and faster and faster)

Reef – Noose – Reef – Noose.
Blood Knot – Bowline – Clove Hitch – Granny.
Overhand – Rolling Hitch – Carrick Bend – Monkey Fist.
Running Bowline – Spanish Bowline – Figure of 8 –
    Fishermen's Bend.

Splicing and cleating and coiling and heaving.
Jamming and slipping and kinking and sealing.
Whipping and seizing. Whipping and seizing.
    Cotton or hemp, manila or twine. Rise and shine!
    There's always a knot at the end of the line!

After two years as a scout, I remained fifth in a patrol of six. I was much more of a liability than an asset, and I knew it.

If I sound Eeyore-ish about this, it's because I greatly admire the all-rounder. In England and Minnesota, I have friends who are distinguished scholars, distinguished artists who have also built the houses they live in with their own hands, or created medieval gardens; who sail boats; who are technophiles. My grandfather Frank was a marvellous carpenter; my mother and father used their hands. So why am I so unpractical? Why do I regard the smallest achievement as tantamount to reaching base camp on Mount Everest?

At the end of the summer term, the Swanbourne pack or troop or whatever it was went away to scout camp. This concentrated and mandatory week was a different matter altogether from our weekly meetings, and I was worried about it.

My fears were not unfounded. As soon as each patrol had pitched its tents, I was detailed to help dig the shit-pits, or the 'latrines' as the scoutmaster elegantly called them, and I worked with such a will that I raised bubble-blisters at the base of my delicate viola-playing fingers. Then it was back to our patrol area where my peers had gathered a decent pile of twigs and sticks.

We were issued with two sausages and an egg each, and with

a frying pan and a matchbox containing only two matches.

The sky turned sickly yellow-and-grey; wind gusted through the diseased elms. It began to rain.

Was it partly because I was so unpractical that my parents later chose to send me to a school that put such emphasis on self-reliance? Where students learned to work for much of the time on their own and where, each week, time was allocated for pioneering (largely estate maintenance)? Where they began each day with a dip into a cold bath and went for brisk pre-breakfast walks and wore shorts, summer and winter alike? Where the regime was, if not spartan, anyhow bracing?

When one of the two scoutmasters did the rounds in the gloom and peppered (or rather, sugared) us with clichés such as 'What rough luck!' and 'Tomorrow's another day', and 'When the going gets tough, the tough get going', he also reminded us not to touch the insides of our tents, otherwise the rain would come through.

'There's a limit to what waterproofing can do,' he said.

There was.

Next morning, I dismally constructed a sort of railing of sticks beside the smoky fire, and draped my sodden pyjamas over them. Then the railing fell forward.

Whatever I put my hand to blistered me or blew out or leaked or fell apart or got smoked.

All this, and it was still early in the morning of our first full day.

It's easy enough to make fun of the Scout Movement with its woggles and dib-dib-dibs and badges, but that's not my intention. Despite its decline during the 1990s from its earlier huge popularity and massive jamborees, one can scarcely argue with its underlying purpose 'of instructing boys of all classes in the principles of discipline, loyalty and good citizenship'. Well, one can argue with the sexism but, since 2007, all Scout Groups in Britain have been open to girls too.

I dare say I learned more than I think. I enjoyed map-reading. I relished scout's pace – alternating one hundred steps walking and one hundred steps running – and still adopt it on my way down to the village, or even around the house; I become very impatient, I know, with mumbling and stumbling and slow motion. I mastered the Morse code and knew how to semaphore. And I've always delighted in carefully laying and knowing how to feed a fire, as well as where and when to plant potatoes in the ashes. And then there are those intangibles: a sense of honour, loyalty, independence.

The 'wide games' played by scouts – I think this designation is simply an abbreviation of 'far and wide' – are really no more than extensions of games such as Grandmother's Footsteps and Hide-and-Seek and Sardines played by younger children, and like them they involve stealth, pursuit, evasion, capture and fear.

On the second day, the weather took a turn for the better, and that afternoon we played an ambitious wide game. Each member of our patrol secured a scarlet cotton tab to his khaki shirt with a safety-pin. Just below the right shoulder. And the other patrols fixed tabs to their shoulders, sky-blue and yellow, black, burgundy and grass-green.

One of our two scoutmasters, a rather stunted chap with an extravagant moustache, unrolled a large-size map and showed us the extensive area, perhaps a square mile, within which we were to play the game.

Then the other, a man with ferocious bifocals and a bark worse than his bite, explained that the object of the game was to capture as many tabs as possible, and told us which patrol was chasing which. 'As soon as you're touched,' he said, 'you're captured, and you must hand over your tab. The patrol that comes back with the most tabs will be the winners. I'll give three long blasts on this whistle to begin the game, and three to end it.'

The clouds cleared; the July afternoon grew hot.

Proceeding at scout's pace to the designated area, I was filled with apprehension. It wasn't that I feared the rough-and-tumble of it: it was the prolonged suspense, and dreading that I would once more let my patrol down.

When I saw the theatre of action, embracing cornfields and copses and trees and hedges and hummocks and hollows, I immediately hit on a plan. With a caution most would call cowardice, I decided to go to ground.

As soon as the six patrols had taken their positions around the perimeter, I simply dropped on to my hands and knees and burrowed my way deep into the barley field.

Three distant, piercing blasts, three screams almost. Then heat and silence.

But no, not silence. Grasshoppers chafed their legs; bluebottles buzzed; now and then a wasp fizzed past; a lark sang its astounding descants; and welcome mouthfuls of wind breathed in the field's golden throat.

Some while ago, I read an account of how the transition from hand to mechanised harvesting affected field mice and rabbits. They beat a retreat before the roar of the machines until, terrified, they were trapped in the uncut square of corn in the middle of the field. Finally, they had to make a run for it, and were easily picked off by the waiting guns.

My heart palpitated. I itched; I scratched; I sweated. The hot afternoon grew very hot.

But no one came near me.

Nothing ventured, nothing gained. But nothing lost either. Scarcely 'prepared', I know; but at least not unprepared. When the whistle blew, I emerged from my dug-out very pink, very subdued, and for once I bit on my tongue.

Midway through camp, there was a family evening. Parents and siblings drove in and, to my surprise and pleasure, because I thought he'd have to be in London and anyhow usually turned his back on such occasions, I saw my father accompanying my mother and Sally.

When the scoutmaster announced a rounders competition in which each patrol was to be fortified by several parents or siblings, to my astonishment my father offered to play. And to my huge gratification he proceeded to welt the ball all over the place, once clean over a mature conker tree. Scuttling from marker to marker, he scored one full rounder after another.

Neenie had told me that my father had been no mean sprinter as a boy, and had won a long-distance swimming race from Scolt Head to the staithe despite being stung by jellyfish, while I knew he had ball-sense after playing tennis with him, but this was a side of him I had simply never seen before.

I was so thrilled and proud when my patrol won the competition and everyone crowded round and said it was because of my father. In my view, it was an achievement to rank beside the performance of his cantata, *The Sacred Dance*, at the Three Choirs Festival.

What a long reach such moments and revelations have. When my two sons were boys, I strained every sinew on Sports Day in the Fathers' Race and managed to win it several years in succession. It mattered so much to me – more, perhaps, than to them. And when I have played occasional games of rounders with my family on Scolt Head or been to watch a baseball game between the Minnesota Twins and one of their National League opponents, I invariably think of a clearing in the woods, a scout camp, a father who redeemed his son.

> Under the spreading chestnut tree,
> Where I held you on my knee,
> We'll be happy as can be;
> Under the spreading chestnut tree.

Everyone sat down on the long log benches around the fire. The air was misty, and quite chill.

While baked beans bubbled and sausages spat, we began to sing. Bending our elbows and spreading our hands, we all imitated tree branches, we all tapped the tops of our heads and patted our chests, even my father, until half our song was cheerful melody and half gesture.

Beating and Initiation

After a hectic summer holidays that began with scout camp and included the Laurent's tempestuous visit, two weeks in Norfolk, my first golfing lessons (armed with my mother's long-unused, wooden-shafted clubs), cycling pilgrimages to see friends and rub church brasses and, lastly, *faute d'Edinburgh* and its festival (and Naomi!), a trip to Dovedale with my parents and Sally, I returned to Swanbourne for my last year.

I knew I was by no means certain to pass the impending Common Entrance exam, but for all that I did very little to raise my game. The best anyone could say of me was that I might be a late developer. It's also fair to say that my hormones were already racing so fast, and continued to do so for the next ten years, that they vied with my academic work.

While I relished time on the rifle range where I became an averagely good shot with the .22, and spent soft evenings playing tennis on the grass court, and while I actually won the annual cross-country race held at the beginning of the so-called spring term, I did the minimum of deskwork. I was not a 'serious student'; and not 'a quick learn'.

During prep one January evening, I was caught flicking

paper pellets with my ruler at one of my friends. 'Once more,' the duty-master told me, 'and you'll be for the high jump.'

A few minutes later, I was caught gossiping, and sent forthwith to the headmaster's study.

I knew what awaited me. On my way, I quickly went to the masters' lavatory, pulled down my shorts and pants, and stretched my snotty white handkerchief over my bottom.

My timing could not possibly have been worse. There was a swish of air, the door swung open, and in walked Mr Evans.

'What do you think you're doing?' he demanded.

'I was j–just coming to see you, sir,' I stammered.

What I didn't like (who would?) was the waiting, the preparatory stroke that sounded like the ripping of a sheet of paper. But, in itself, being beaten seemed of no great consequence. Sharp it was, but also short, and by no means the most effective deterrent for the majority of young boys. One of my letters refers to how I 'just failed to get beaten', while another casually begins, 'One thing I forgot to tell you yesterday was that I had been beaten a few days previously by Mr Evans in games clothes'!

I'm aware, of course, not only of the potential and documented abuse of beating but of children's differing sensibilities and tolerance of pain. But in the impartial, wholly matter-of-fact way it was administered at Swanbourne, divorced from anger or sexual gratification, I don't believe the cane had any psychological after-effects on me whatsoever. After my first beating, I certainly regarded it as preferable to the interminable, time-wasting occupation of writing lines.

In some ways, I was rather an oddity at Swanbourne. Each Monday evening, the young composer Philip Cannon arrived to give me my viola lesson – this had been arranged by my father, and I was the only pupil learning the instrument. I loved the look of my vintage instrument and lovingly tended it; I listened to my vinyl recording of *Hassan*; and I was excited to meet William Primrose after the first performance of Edmund Rubbra's *Viola Concerto*. But for all this, I struggled to read music. I struggled with tempo (years later, as the speaker in

Walton's *Façade*, I only barely managed to hold my own), and I struggled with technique. For three more years, though, I persisted, playing in my public school's second orchestra. Why? And why was I such a dud? There's a limit to how much one can blame on filial piety.

On some evenings, during the free hour or so after prep and before bedtime, I played chess against my friend Algie Peel, or pressed on with my guide to *Church Brasses in Buckinghamshire*, or reread my battered old copy of *Our Island Story* for the umpteenth time; and from time to time I walked over to the chapel, and in the moonlight got down on my knees and prayed silent prayers. I remember the great intensity of these occasions, but not what my prayers were about.

Early in 1954, I wrote a couple of poems, maybe my first. Ominously entitled 'Life' and 'Peace', one is a dire religious diatribe against the evildoers of the world while the other evokes a scene in which a cat is lying asleep beside a burning fire and a grandfather clock is ticking. It ends:

> The crimson carpet glows as if in joy.
> Once again the music swells and diminishes
> But I am just a boy
> Just another dream finishes.

True, our English homework occasionally entailed writing a short story, but my only other voluntary literary endeavour at Swanbourne was 'The Deathly Room: No. 21', a contribution to the eight-headed *Set 4 Ghost Stories*, written the previous year. The narrative cracks along well enough, but it has very little imaginative kick or feeling for language.

On one winter evening, I decided to vary my diet by writing to the new Queen – and I kept a copy of the letter I wrote to her:

My Dear Majesty,

I expect you get every stamp ever issued, so I wonder wheather you could get me one or two ~~two~~ stamps, and also your autograph and any more the Royal family could spare the time and are at home.

Yours affectionately

Kevin Crossley-Holland

P.S. Please do not wory if you cannot spare the time.

I can't remember whether or not I received a reply from one of the Queen's ladies-in-waiting but if so, there were no enclosures!

During my last year, I slept in an altogether larger dormitory. True, I was now delivered from the sweet attentions of Licker Lonsdale, but where nine or ten twelve-year-old boys on the threshold of adolescence are gathered together . . .

We bounced on our beds until the springs separated; we flicked our tie-ends at one another until they began to unravel; we had pillow-fights and rough-and-tumbles; we had cockfights – the first to grasp his opponent's bare cock was the winner; and then, after lights-out, many a boy lay on his back, knees raised, and the tent of his bed shook and throbbed. I was mystified by this.

'They're masturbating,' said Jack Ramply, who slept in the bed next to mine.

'Whatting?'

'Masturbating! Morbus, it feels wonderful.'

'What do you do?'

When Jack discovered how innocent I was, he realised he could profit from it. And so, for the price of no less than two Sundays' worth of sweets – five ounces, that's to say – he taught me.

During the winter term, my parents had to address the question of where to send me after Swanbourne, and how to afford it.

I think it was immediately after Christmas that we went to look round quite cordial, formal, exam-conscious Westminster School (I had been 'put down' for both Westminster and Eton at birth), and soon after that we drove up to Gresham's School in Norfolk where the headmaster told us that senior boys were allowed pets, and later delighted my mother by showing us a small courtyard with a pond in it, and observing that 'This is where the boys who bring crocodiles keep their crocodiles.'

With its pastoral strength and association with a medieval guild (the Fishmongers), my parents were attracted to Gresham's. And so was I. More than forty years later, their mother Gillian and I sent our two daughters Oenone and Eleanor there for their A-level years.

Back at school it turned very cold. Between classes, many of us stood with our backs to the grunting, blisteringly hot radiators. In the evenings, we began to rehearse for the school production of *She Stoops to Conquer*. Having failed to impress as Faulkland in the previous year's production, *The Rivals*, I had a very minor part as Pimple, a rather pretty maidservant.

Not that servants, tutors, nurses and the like always have minor parts. When I was sixteen, I played the significant role of the messenger in Seneca's *The Troades*, and had to run on to the stage (slither, actually, in a rain-afflicted open-air production in a Greek theatre), bringing devastating news of fire and destruction, crying '*O dura fata! Saeva! Miseranda! Horrida!*'

One January weekend, standing water was covered with a thick lid of ice, and the entire school, eighty or ninety of us, were taken in coaches to a small mere. None of us had skates, and few knew how to skate, but we spent a couple of delirious hours there, slipping and sliding and shoving and shouting.

A day or two later, my mother wrote to Mr Evans saying that she and my father had decided against both Westminster and Gresham's, and that after Christmas, at the beginning of the spring term, they would like to take me down to a school in the south-west of England.

A school, my father told me, with the motto '*Et nova et vetera*'.

'New and old,' I said.

'*Both* new *and* old,' my father corrected me. 'Words of good omen.'

Ice and Flame

As a teenager, my mother became interested in astronomy and so, typically enough, she wrote to the Astronomer Royal, Sir Frank Dyson, to declare her interest and ask him a few pertinent questions. The Astronomer Royal replied, and before long they were engaged in regular correspondence that lasted until my mother was into her twenties.

When I was seven or eight, she gave me a pocket guide to astronomy. Sometimes we stood on the verandah at Crosskeys and stared at the night sky. Stared deep into it, until I could recognise at least some of the constellations.

For my father, the heavens were primarily a matter of reverence and the music of the spheres; for my mother, an ever-changing sky-field that inspired practical investigation.

Since myths invariably contain features of the physical region in which they're created, it's not surprising that one Norse creation myth describes how, in the huge emptiness of Ginnungagap, fire from the south meets ice from the north and, as the ice melts, life quickens: 'Burning ice, biting flame; that is how life began.'

We experience this same duality, the fiery and the freezing, when we contemplate the night sky. At times I gazed up, magnetised, and my imagination ran wild; at times it all became too much, fearsome in its immensity, and I retreated indoors.

Dramatising our childhoods, we bypass the humdrum, and conflate or concertina different moments into one in much the same way as the sound of the gong combines many different notes. Thus, my winter holidays cannot have consisted exclusively of expeditions to the steep snowy slopes at the end of the lane but neither did it consist of a single glorious outing. So all I can offer, more than half a century later, is a distillation.

Overnight, there has been a great snowfall. And now, before dawn, the snow stops, it grows colder, and Jack Frost sneaks up and scrawls all over my window. On Sally's window, he leaves beautiful, mysterious patterns.

The first problem is not so much to wake my father – we do that repeatedly – as to convince him that we're not going to let him go back to sleep, and that he really might as well get up. The second is to persuade him to set aside his work and come lugeing with us, and that it will only be 'fun' if he comes.

The truth, I suppose, is that Sally and I both craved more of our father's attention, more of his love. For most of the time, he was not at home, while from the age of ten onwards I was away at school; and even during those holiday weekends, he absented himself for long hours, working in his study.

Now, my mother checks that we're warmly dressed, and wearing second pairs of socks. We unhook the luge from the back of the garage, and we're off.

At the end of the unmade road, there are two fields, one above the other, with a quite small gap in the hedge between them.

Somehow cramming ourselves on to one luge, all three of us career down the top field, steer through the gap without losing speed, hiss down into the lower field until it pans and levels out in front of us.

We roll over into the snow, blow out our pink cheeks, laugh; we chew the liquorice allsorts my father suddenly produces from his fawn windcheater; we gaze west across the misty, frozen Vale of Aylesbury, turn and set our sights on the heights again . . .

Those hours! They were so uncomplicated (unlike, say, my singing lessons); so much a matter of action and not of intellect; so joyous.

There was a time when ice and flame drew close in our little unmade road.

One snowy evening I walked back through the village after dark, trying to visualise the Milky Way as a massive swarm of snowflakes that had, so to speak, fallen upwards and settled on the sky, one of many unscientific, myth-making ways in which I tried to explain the world to myself.

Before I reached Crosskeys, I could see the glow further down Westfield Road, and when I rounded the corner I realised at once that a house was on fire. I ran down to it and found the owners and a dozen or so people watching it, aghast and helpless, waiting for the fire brigade to come.

The energy of a bonfire can be exhilarating. A burning hayrick generates such heat and makes such a noise as to be terrifying. But a house on fire! That's a different matter altogether, because it's built not only of bricks and mortar but dreams, memories, stories, and contains our personal belongings.

I stood alone. I watched the blaze, and seeing how the snow around it melted and the flames were reflected in the standing pools of water, I felt utterly desolate.

In the middle of the field opposite that house, there was a large telegraph pole. As a boy, I loved to go and sit against it, and listen to it humming. I thought its hum consisted of all the telephone conversations being conducted down it, and then made up what some of those conversations were. Just snatches of them. Dramatic and humdrum; careering, considered; words of ice, words of flame.

Lifting my Eyes

Next to Crosskeys, there was a bungalow. That was where Miss Lloyd lived, the retired teacher to whom Sally and I had entrusted ourselves on the night we ran away. And next to Miss Lloyd lived old Mrs Hurst. She believed in fairies. Not only that, she could see them inside her house, and sometimes warned us not to plump ourselves down on a chair or sofa because a fairy was already sitting on it.

Both Miss Lloyd and Mrs Hurst were keen gardeners with very well-stocked gardens and, when I was nine or ten and as usual strapped for cash, I hit on a plan.

This combined theft, cowardice and duplicity in equal measures. First, I got Sally to steal into the two gardens while I kept watch, and pick an armful of flowers. These I covered with a pullover and carried a few yards back up the lane to our kitchen garden. There, Sally and I trimmed and tied them into small bunches, and then, armed with a money-box, the kind you post money into, we walked along the village street, knocking on the doors of anyone we didn't already know, saying we were selling flowers to collect money 'for the poor children'.

'Which poor children?' one woman asked me. A nasty moment.

I told the woman I didn't know and that I'd ask my mother.

'And come back and tell me,' the woman said.

I didn't.

Otherwise, however, this venture was highly successful. So much so we decided to do it again.

This time, though, we went a step too far. Running out of neighbours, we tried – or, more precisely, obedient Sally tried – to sell Miss Lloyd a bunch of her own flowers.

Hidden behind a bush, I heard Miss Lloyd greeting Sally and then saying brightly, 'They look just like mine.'

My mother sent me up to my room for the remainder of the day, and I had to eat my supper alone there. This made me so indignant that I locked her out so she was unable to come in and kiss me good night.

I hope Sally didn't get it in the neck as well. As so often, I was the ringleader, and Sally my loyal slave.

How contained and relatively safe our lives were. Our quiet lane, leading to the fields where we luged and tobogganed, was a dead end, ideal for children to play in. Everyone watched out for one another. And even when Sally and I were sitting on top of the Cross, four hundred feet above her, my mother said she could sometimes hear us singing or calling to each other, and we could hear her when she rang her Alpine cowbell.

Once, my mother lost her diamond-and-ruby ring, inherited from her mother. Search for it as we all did, it had completely disappeared. A few days later, the milkman left it on the doorstep on top of one of our daily pints of milk; he had picked it up on the gravel path just inside our gate.

Within Crosskeys, meanwhile, my mother made much out of relatively little. The brass and silver shone, tabletops gleamed and, with the very fine eye she later brought to the running of the Oxford Gallery, she displayed our few pictures and pots to striking effect.

To begin with, not all the places she installed them were

practical. But after I had knocked over and chipped a beautiful Chinese jade mug while chasing Sally round the lounge, everything valuable was put out of reach.

The circular coal scuttle painted by gipsies in vibrant yellow, royal blue and holly-leaf green; my mother's own pots, some stoneware, some glazed sky-blue, duck-egg blue, forget-me-not; two Bernard Leach tiles; my father's Welsh harp; the stone finial that had fallen off the tower of Soulbury church; a calendar in its silver frame: each had its appointed place within the circle, at once charmed and hapless, of our pretty little Chiltern cottage.

In his study, meanwhile, my father composed graceful rounds (he dedicated these to me, and presented me with the score) and fine songs, some of which number amongst his best work. One of them was a setting of Robert Bridges's 'Nightingales':

> Our song is the voice of desire, that haunts our dreams,
> A throe of the heart . . .

I was not to know that this passionate song, with its 'dark nocturnal secret' and 'raptured ear' and withdrawing, and welcoming of the dawn, was composed for the soprano with whom my father was deeply in love.

Sally has told me our mother went to confront this woman. I don't know where or when, but I can guess why. She would have invited her, calmly, quite warmly, to consider all she was threatening or destroying, but in particular Sally's and my happiness. My mother's bravery made no difference, but cancer soon did. The soprano died a painful death.

The years passed; I lifted my eyes. Sitting at my small desk and staring out of the window, I could see deep into the heart of the Vale of Aylesbury. Now, the names of all the moats and medieval villages, the hamlets, farms and backwaters I cycled to are like a charm: Armour Farm and Quakers Farm and Lane End in Meadle, Kimble Wick and Dinton Castle, Owlswick,

Moreton, Tifnams . . .

Cycling, and driving with my mother to churches 'a little green with holy mildew' to rub brasses, and to-ing and fro-ing between Whiteleaf and Swanbourne, my horizons grew. I felt at home all over Buckinghamshire, and on the grounds that both schools were within easy reach, my parents toyed with the idea of sending me to Stowe or else to Bradfield.

Not for long, though. They had heard from friends about Bryanston, a school where self-reliance was an article of faith, and the visual and performing arts were prized. Even though there were no places left for September 1954, they resolved to take me to see it.

On a sparkling late January morning, the four of us piled into BTM812 and headed for Dorset.

Before we reached Salisbury, my father told me that we were near the heart of Neolithic Britain, not at all far from Stonehenge and Avebury and the chambered barrow known as Wayland's Smithy. 'It's on the Ridgeway,' he told me, 'and after the Ridgeway has crossed the Thames, it becomes our Icknield Way.'

As we drove over Cranborne Chase, it felt as if we were entering another country. Our road unbent and arrowed over the sweeping downs, altogether more empty and unwooded than the secretive Chilterns. Then we passed prehistoric burial mounds, an Iron Age hill fort, signs to a Roman villa . . .

Without explaining himself, my father left the main road at Pentridge and headed south.

'You'll see,' he said.

What we saw was a church the size of a small cathedral in a little market town: Wimborne Minster.

My father led us into the sanctuary where, on the wall, there was a small fifteenth-century brass put up in honour of Ethelred the Unready (*unræd* actually means un- or ill-advised), buried at Wimborne in 1016.

'It's the only royal brass there is,' my father told me.

Quite how he knew this, I have no idea.

Perhaps he'd been to Wimborne before, because he then

drove us out of the town, and along a two-mile avenue of mature beech trees to the Iron Age hill fort of Badbury Rings. Once, there were three hundred and sixty-five trees on one side and three hundred and sixty-six on the other, but normal years and leap years alike have diminished their ranks.

My father stopped the car and looked over his shoulder at me. 'Some people say this is Mons Badonicus,' he said.

'What's Badonicus?' asked Sally.

'Mount Badon,' my father said. 'Kevin knows.'

I did know. Mount Badon was the last of the twelve great battles in which the Britons, led perhaps by Arthur, fought and defeated the Anglo-Saxons. What was my father up to? Was he making connections, involving me in Dorset's layers, helping me to feel at ease before we arrived on the doorstep?

Doorstep, however, is a misnomer and much too cosy. A very grand arch and a gatehouse; a drive more than two miles long; an immense, gravelled courtyard; the many doors of the vast brick-and-stuccoed mansion that once belonged to Lord Portman.

I think I fell in love with Bryanston at first sight – its magnificent Greek Theatre, its hills and its extensive woods, its Sculpture and Pottery rooms. And I loved the graceful River Stour despite the ominous prospect of having to take the 'second river test', and swim from bank to bank, fully clothed.

It was only later that I fell under the spell of the school's ethos (to develop individuality and self-discipline, to fit students to serve the community), an aim wonderfully expressed by its wise and compassionate headmaster, Thorold Coade:

> It is not merely to teach boys how to pass examinations; it is not primarily even to give them knowledge; it is to awaken them, where necessary, to the innumerable possibilities of life . . . We need to cultivate the attitude of the artist. The artist regards his subject, and the problems it presents – his model, his landscape, his still-life group – not as things with which he can cope only with great difficulty, or things to be created or represented on canvas

or in stone or wood. He regards them as material for creation – material for his own creative genius to accept and use in order to reveal the absolute values, truth and beauty. So we, if we are to live creatively, must accept life, welcome life, with all its snags, hardship, tragedy – as the material out of which we are challenged to make something new – a new world.*

All I remember of my interview with Mr Coade, said to be one of the two outstanding headmasters of his generation (Roxburgh of Stowe was the other), was that when he asked me about my hobbies, I was completely tongue-tied. I couldn't think of anything. Not my museum. Not church brass-rubbing. Not playing tennis. My mother must surely have rehearsed me in what not to say, but it may never have occurred to her that my anxiety would deprive me of my memory and strike me dumb.

Mr Coade was patient. He coaxed me. And eventually, only too aware of how much this interview mattered, I remembered that I collected stamps. 'The British Empire,' I said, 'and Switzerland and the Vatican City.'

The next week, when I was back at Swanbourne, Thorold Coade wrote to my parents. He thanked them for bringing me down, and said he had liked meeting me. He reiterated that there were no available places for September 1954, but went on to say there was often a last-minute cancellation or two. Provided, he wrote, that I passed my Common Entrance exam, he would do his best to find a place for me.

My mother took that to be a yes.

'If you do go,' Harold Evans told me, 'you'll be the first from Swanbourne to do so.' He stretched his neck.

I could hear the challenge in his voice, and the proviso. I resolved to work harder.

---

* *The Burning Bow: A Selection from the Papers of T. F. Coade of Bryanston* (1966).

Common Entrance

The Common Entrance exam consisted of twelve papers, most of them forty-five or sixty minutes long. Candidates were instructed that 'Ball-pointed pens should not be used in this examination.'

But in which room did I sit them? With whom did I discuss them? And how did I feel about them? Strangely, I have no memory whatsoever of taking these exams, so long prepared for and so crucial. So all I can do is give a flavour of them.

The first subject on 21 June was English A, and it tested our powers of description, précis, grammatical construction and clarity of thought. The first question, making assumptions about car ownership and foreign travel, and acknowledging the superiority of the French railway system, was as follows:

A French train recently attained a speed of 150 miles an hour on a stretch of its regular run. You were waiting in your father's car to cross the line at a level-crossing when the train passed.

Write about a page describing what you saw and heard.

Then came the first Latin paper, testing our vocabulary,

grammar and ability to translate from English into Latin and vice versa; and, before lunch, there was a Scripture paper, examining our knowledge, comprehension and opinions. For instance: 'With what outstanding event in the history of the Christian Church do you connect the Feast of Pentecost? Show briefly why you think it was, and is, so important to the Church.'

After lunch, we switched from the humanities to the sciences (Arithmetic and Geometry), while the next day brought Algebra, History and Geography and after lunch, French A and B. In the History exam, I see that I elected to 'Tell the story of any one baronial rebellion in the Middle Ages – its causes, events and results'. Shades of *Our Island Story*! In Geography, I drew a sketch map of Wales and related what I knew about Kenya, Monsoons, the International Date Line and Night and Day.

On the third day examinees tackled the demanding last two papers. The Latin B paper further tested our ability to translate from Latin into English and English into Latin. English B, meanwhile, called for critical understanding of verses from Macaulay's *Horatius*, invited us to write a short essay arguing for and against the proposition that 'the next war will not be between *nations*; it will be between *planets*', and asked us to suggest suitable words to fill the blanks in the following passage from *Lorna Doone*:

And now in (1) plight I came to an opening in the bushes, where a great (2) pool lay in front of me. I shuddered and drew back, not alone at the pool itself and the black(3) there was about it but also at its whirling manner and the (4) of white threads upon it, in (5) circles round and round, and the (6) still as jet. I soon saw the reason for the stir and depth of that great pit. For (7) round one side (with very little comfort because the rocks were high and (8) and the (9) at the foot so narrow) I came to a sudden sight and marvel such as I had never dreamed of. I stood at the foot of a long (10) slide of water coming smoothly towards me without any break for a hundred yards or more, straight and shining, as if it had been combed or (11) and looking like a (12) of deal laid down a deep black stair-case.

I filled in the blanks as follows: (1) a, (2) black, (3) look, (4) number, (5) revolving, (6) centre, (7) scrambling, (8) jagged, (9) width, (10) silent, (11) bestilled, (12) plank.

I'm stunned by the level of questions in this set of common or garden Common Entrance papers. Had I been taking the Scholarship exam to Bryanston, I would also have been invited to sit papers in Music, Music Practical, Art Practical, Science, Latin Verse, Greek (two papers) and German. I'm no educationalist but I cannot think expectations are as high now as they were in 1954.

All my papers were forwarded to Bryanston, and before the end of term Harold Evans was informed that I had 'been successful in the Examination for Entrance'. My best papers were Arithmetic and Latin A, in each of which I achieved 88 per cent, and my least successful Algebra B and Geometry B (40 per cent in each case).

No less strange than my inability to remember taking these exams is the fact that for most of my adult years, I believed that I failed them, and often told people as much.

Did I consciously bend the facts to make a good story and then end up believing the story myself? Or was the whole experience of taking Common Entrance so fraught that my memory subsequently changed fear of failure into failure itself?

Certainly, the results were delayed and there was some upsetting hiccup in communications between Bryanston, Swanbourne and my parents. But what exactly, I do not know.

'So now, Kevin,' said Mr Evans, 'it's in the lap of the gods.'

'Sorry, sir?'

'You've kept your part of the bargain. You've passed CE. Now it's a matter of whether or not Bryanston can find a place for you.'

Happy Families

When, at Ian Agnew's birthday party, we were told we were going to play Murder, the nape of my neck froze and tingled. I couldn't wait for the 'game' to begin; I couldn't wait for it to end. Each of us drew a card, taking care not to show anyone else what it was, and the one with the Ace of Spades was the murderer, while the one who drew the Ace of Hearts was the detective. Then we all panned out through the house and the lights were turned off. At once the tension grew. And grew. By the time one guest was told in a whisper that he or she was the victim and, the regulation ten seconds later, screamed and fell to the ground, I found it almost unbearable. At once the house lights were turned on again and everyone was obliged to remain standing exactly where they were while the detective did the rounds, inspected the crime scene, and so on.

After this, we all gathered in one room and, when the detective questioned us, we were each allowed to lie three times. This part of the game was social – a matter of wits, a poker face, laughter. But I still felt as if I'd just emerged from the most appalling nightmare, no less frightening than my dream of being chased by the long-haired witch through the forest to the pencil-thin tower, or conducting my small daughters through the dreadful ghost-house at the Minnesota State Fair, unable in the grey gloom to protect them from bony, sudden-snatching fingers.

Most party games, however, challenged our dexterity or speed or memory or general knowledge, not our nervous systems.

One that I rather liked but never won was Kim's Game in which one stares silently for a couple of minutes at twenty or so small objects laid out on a tray, and then tries to remember and list them. And one game that fascinated me was attempting to recognise well-known people (very few of us had television) from newspaper photographs of parts of their faces.

In Norfolk and at home, we had two favourite games. With Neenie, it was mah-jong. She loved building the four walls with her clacking porcelain tiles, and did so with the greatest care, as if she were laying the foundations for her own cottage. Whenever she could, she collected exotic red and white dragons – later, I discovered that while dragons are ferocious enemies in north-west European mythology and legend, Chinese dragons are benign, and bringers of rain. But above all, Neenie treasured the green dragons that matched her beautiful Coalport crockery. She turned her back on the winds.

'We've plenty enough of those as it is, boy,' she told me.

At home, meanwhile, my mother produced games she had safely stored away since she was a girl, such as Pelmanism and Indoor Croquet. But Sally's and my favourite was the pacific card game in which you simply ask one of the other participants whether he or she has a certain card, with the aim of building up fictional families of four.

Happy Families is one of the many games, including Snakes and Ladders, Tiddlywinks and Ludo, said to have been invented during the first part of the nineteenth century by John Jaques, and the semi-caricatures on the original cards are attributed to Sir John Tenniel, first illustrator of *Alice's Adventures in Wonderland*.

Time and again, my mother and father obligingly played with us as we cheerfully collected Mr Bones the Butcher and Mrs Soot the Sweep's wife, Master Dose the Doctor's son and Miss Snuffet the Undertaker's daughter.

I remember them all, on their thick, cream, almost square matt cards: Mr Hearty the Captain and Mrs Tuckin the Chef's wife, Miss Bud the Florist's daughter and Master Chalk the Teacher's son. But a happy family is what we were not. This is the game the four of us played, and none of us could win.

Leafing through my mother's albums, I'm struck by how so very few photographs portray her and my father alone together, and taken aback by the physical space between them in group photographs. Stiff or tight-lipped; separated by a third party; one leaning forward, the other in the background; turning away from one another. These are painful pictures for a son to look at, and I keep wondering how I failed to see then what I see so plainly now.

Certainly, I remember wondering why my parents slept in separate beds, but did I never question their lack of day-to-day fondness and physical affection? This failure, at any rate, is precisely what they wished for. In a way, my blindness is proof of their success.

It is not for me to judge whether they were right or wrong in deciding to maintain their marriage until Sally and I were more or less grown up, but I later regretted and deplored it. Often I talk to myself about the price of repression. About sacrifice and fulfilment. About how above all we must show our children that we love them.

Happy Families was the child of a society and time in which the *pater familias* supported his virtually unbreakable family, his wife maintained the household, and their children were miniature replicas, to be seen and largely not heard. My mother and my father both came from Victorian middle-class families that in part conformed to this patriarchal model, and they both paid a price for it.

Every Man Needs a Tool

One afternoon during the last week of the summer term, Mr Evans summoned the school leavers to his study. We all knew what this was about. Sex.

There were seventeen of us. Like a swarm of grey locusts we settled on the chaise-longue, the armchairs and, in uncomfortable proximity, all over the floor.

The headmaster picked his way between us across the room and opened the French windows (shades of Gerard Hoffnung, the extremely funny musician and humorist whom my father never found in the least funny) that were already misting over with so much heavy breathing.

Then Mrs Evans arrived bearing a plate of crumbly cakes. Deeming her husband's study to be part of her fastidious house and not part of the school, she looked down at us through her pince-nez with exquisite distaste. Then she offered each of us a cake, and warned us, 'Be careful of the crumbs!'

'Let them eat cake,' a scholarship boy volunteered. 'Let them eat cake.'

Mrs Evans's eyes glittered, and she bestowed on him a thin-lipped smile.

We wolfed the cakes. Mrs Evans withdrew.

The headmaster looked round the room.

'Right!' he began. 'Now we all have this Thing.'

At this juncture, I was still not wholly clear about the function of this Thing. I knew it felt tender and I knew it was private. I knew I peed with it and had taken part in 'Who can pee the furthest?' contests. I knew it had something to do with making babies. And, thanks to Jack Ramply, I knew how to masturbate.

'This Thing,' repeated the headmaster. 'I call it a Tool.'

All around me, I could hear the silence deepening.

'Tool! There's no need to be ashamed of it. Every man needs a Tool.'

Sensitive and even witty though Mr Evans was, I found my first sex lecture excruciating. I wished there were more space around me on the study floor. As soon as it was all over, the seventeen of us self-consciously hurried out through the French windows and sprayed all over the school grounds. We climbed tall trees (strictly one boy per tree) and, keeping companionable silence, sat on high for a long time to cool off.

On the last morning of term, I was detailed to raise the flag on the mast that stood in one corner of the gravel courtyard, in front of dismal Scout Wood. Demob happy, I left the scout flag folded, tied a chamber-pot to the rope and raised that instead.

This was not a good idea. The headmaster came and found me himself and, with a sinking stomach, I followed him back to his study. Mr Evans asked me whether I thought I'd been funny, belittling the school and insulting the parents. Then he beat me.

I thought then that I deserved what I got. But couldn't the headmaster have treated a prank as a prank, and sent me packing from Swanbourne with a flea in my ear, not with three stripes on my bum?

In Norfolk: Time, Tide and Tennis

A couple of days after I left Swanbourne, my parents posted me up to Norfolk for a few days on my own with Neenie and Grandpa Frank.

My father and I took the train from Princes Risborough to Marylebone, and then the Underground via King's Cross to Liverpool Street Station, and I marvelled at having touched on three Monopoly stations in such a short space of time. It made London manageable.

At the barrier, I said goodbye to my father. He never gave me a hug or anything like that, but just clasped my right hand with both of his, and sometimes laid a friendly hand on my shoulder. So I put my prep school days behind me. I left my mother and father at home. The world was my oyster:

> The terminus smells of wild garlic,
> The buttoned cloth is squirrel red-brown.
> There are depths as black as black holes
> where the barley has been beaten down.
> The caparisoned elms are alight
> (Each stilled in a flood of gold fire).
> Such dawdles! Standstills! The white

skyline is lanced by a crocketed spire.
Wild roses cling to pink brick. The track
is burning sienna. Almost, almost free!
Beyond the hectares of mangel and beet
Open silver-grey arms, stunning, the sea.*

The main line carried me as far as King's Lynn, and from there I took a smaller train. At coiffured Wolferton, the station for Sandringham, described by Betjeman as 'different from all other stations in England', I saw the crowns on the lamp-posts and red carpet stretched along the platform; at Heacham, I looked for signs of the Great Flood, but it's not always easy to detect absences; and at Hunstanton, Alan Bell, who ran an occasional taxi service, was waiting to meet me.

The line from King's Lynn (or Lynn, as it once was) to Hunst'n no longer exists. And neither does the line that meandered from Hunst'n through Docking and Stanhoe to Burnham Market. I took it several times, and on each Norfolk visit for many years went to inspect the giant green locomotive beached in the back yard of Mason's Garage. But then, in 1963, the stopping-train stopped once and for all. Almost half a century later, the image of the axeman Dr Beeching is firmly enshrined in the chamber of modern monsters. Folk memory is a terrible thing!

On the way to Overy Staithe, Alan told me about his fights as an amateur boxer. Somehow I assumed they'd gone on until one man could no longer get up from his corner, and asked Alan what was the most number of rounds he'd fought.

He smiled. 'I may look old,' he said.

At this moment, a preening cock pheasant got in the way of his taxi. Before I was even sure what had happened, Alan jumped out, opened the boot and popped the pheasant into it.

Once, while driving Sally and me to see friends near Little Missenden, prettiest of names, my mother ran over a tabby cat. We pulled up and looked out of the rear window and saw

* *Selected Poems*: 'On the Way East'.

the cat springing into the air. Vertically. Shrieking and spring-ing, five or six times. For once, my mother didn't know what to do; or, knowing that the only thing to do was to run over the cat a second time, couldn't bring herself to do it. She ran up the path of the nearby cottage to find the owners.

That episode seared me, and I still feel the cat's pain more fiercely than my own with a fishhook in my thumb or a slate in my shin, perhaps because we inflicted it, or because we were unable to do anything about it.

As a boy, my Slazenger tennis racquets were wooden-framed and strung not with nylon but with so-called cat-gut – only much later did I discover the gut came from sheep or other livestock, never from cats. It's no exaggeration to say that every time I played tennis for the next few years, I thought again about that luckless Missenden cat.

In Norfolk, I sometimes played tennis against pretty Eileen, one of Alan Bell's adult daughters. But the Great Flood had chewed up the hardcourt, just as it had overrun and eaten into the swimming-pool of the Moorings Hotel.

But after a week or so my parents and Sally drove up to join me in our new deluxe saloon Volkswagen Beetle (BTM812 had passed away at last) and, almost immediately, I took part in the Norfolk Junior Tennis Tournament in Hunstanton.

How eager I was. And how anxious. Once, I ran right round the net to pick up a couple of balls my opponent had served into it. In the event, I was very quickly put out of my misery without, as Bill Frindle says, 'troubling the scorer'.

This was my first tournament, and the way in which I can remember it and subsequent school matches, set for set, some of them game for game, speaks for itself. The last time my mother and I played each other – I don't know why she 'retired' so early – was during this same holiday. Fierce and fair, she had a lovely flowing backhand, as natural as yawning or stretching. She beat me 6-2, 6-4, and when I ran forward to congratulate her, I bounced against the net and snapped it. Yes, once I aced Sangster, and once I played doubles against the pair who represented Ireland in the Davis Cup, but no amount of 'onces' make a summer. My tennis was as often social as seriously competitive, and never more so than when, aged eighteen, I returned to teach at Swanbourne for just one term before going up to Oxford, and played an evening game against a lovely young woman. We were avidly watched by at least half the school, forty boys or so, all of them wearing pyjamas, concealed in the surrounding shrubbery!

Eager and anxious, yes, and impressionable too. In Norfolk, I read Malcolm Saville's *Redshanks Warning*, and the descriptions of smugglers sending signals across the saltmarsh from the Beacon Tower of Blakeney church so excited me that, even now, I never drive past the church without thinking of it. Before long, we all went to see the tower, as well as the smugglers' cottage in Brancaster Staithe, said to be connected to a little marshy islet by a tunnel. This is one of the least likely of the improbable tunnel stories connecting England underground much as a web of shining railtracks once connected it on the surface.

With Grandpa Frank, I attended an auction of paintings by his neighbour and friend, Gwen Salmond (Lady Matthew Smith). My grandfather 'opened' the auction with choice words and a starting bid of £1 for the first lot. He then took no further part in the proceedings, and that struck me, and still does, as mean.

With Neenie, we played mah-jong and went to the annual fair set up on the Hard beside the creek. For some reason the owners entirely misjudged the height of the tide and, on a calm, sunlit early July evening, all the stalls were flooded. But this didn't deter the stallholders and it didn't deter people living or holidaying in the Burnhams. Joyously, we all splashed around in water that came up to our knees and, before long, softened the marl on the Hard and made it slimy. We threw darts; we shot at the procession of plastic yellow ducks; we rolled pennies; we launched rings that never, ever snared prizes; the only stall that threw in the towel, so to speak, was the coconut shy.

It grew dark. The organ ground. Candyfloss spun. Round and round whirled the merry-go-round, and all the coloured lights jigged in the reaching water.

On the Hard and on the marsh path, on the dyke and beach, Sally and I struck up dozens of conversations with children who were holidaying in the Burnhams. But it was difficult to form lasting friendships with any of them because we were our grandparents' guests, and our days were governed by piety and mealtimes, not by tides.

If forewarned, Neenie was prepared to make a picnic lunch for the four of us, but my parents thought it only courteous that on most days we should get back to Rahere for lunch. While our peers were settling into nests in the dunes, and tucking in to their sandwiches, we were trooping back to the staithe, or pushing *Mallard* over intractable sandbars, invariably muddy, invariably late.

On some afternoons, we went on outings with my grandparents, and it's only now, living in North Norfolk, that I realise how prescribed and limited these were. Back to the Shell Museum at Glandford; back to Ringstead Common, and the esplanade at Sheringham and half-a-dozen churches. But why did we break so little new ground? Why did we never visit Holkham Hall or Blickling or the astounding church, made of light and space, at Salle?

As Sally and I were not encouraged to bring back friends to Rahere, we sometimes spent time in their caravans and holiday cottages. Now and then, Joan Robinson, author of *When Marnie Was There*, asked us to stay for supper in their caravan and, during my teens, her daughter Debbie and I became good friends.

Our closest friends, though, were Sally, John and Polly Richter, and their mother Beryl. They lived in Cambridge and always rented 'Sunray', the same bright green LNER carriage, parked by Mason's Garage in Overy Staithe. As I saw it, they were not the least interested in discipline or tidiness, they were disrespectful of authority, they were wilful and outspoken and teased us, and I found them fascinating, almost dangerous. Sally and Polly and Beryl invariably wore slops and kerchiefs and scruffy, brightly coloured clothes and, to my eye, they looked like the gipsies who did the rounds at Whiteleaf, selling wooden pegs and trinkets, and asking whether we had any unwanted shoes. When, once, my mother gave the gipsies a pair of my father's walking shoes, I was shocked.

'Won't Daddy mind?' I asked her.

'He won't have to,' she replied brusquely.

The Richter children were all artistic – in the event, Sally is a poet and biographer, John was a sculptor and letter-carver and is now a fine painter, and Polly is a sculptor – and all three care passionately for North Norfolk.

John told me his father was a famous scientist and lived in Wales.

'Has he come up to Overy?' I asked.

'No.' Then and now, John is not prodigal with words.

'How often can he come home?' I persisted.

'He lives in Cardiff.'

'You mean . . . all the time?'

'They're divorced.'

The parents of some of my friends at Swanbourne must surely have been divorced, but this was the first time I'd come face to face with the beast.

'Can you see him?' I asked.

'Of course,' said John equably. 'We go and stay with him each holidays.'

In Beryl, my mother found a good companion to help her keep a sense of perspective and humour during her summer holidays in Norfolk. Like so many other women, she worshipped my father but, unlike any others, she teased him and never allowed him to take himself seriously.

The Richters were swimmers, sailors, independent loners. They had no time for my growing religious orthodoxy or my love of competition, and derided the way in which all the

Crossley-Hollands spent so much time searching for cornelian. This said, one year we had a family contest on Scolt Head, and John remembers that 'each of us tried to get ahead to find the best piece with the result that we all walked at such a pace that nothing was found at all. What we did find was that we had reached the Hut Hills, further than any of us had been before; then had to face the long trek back.'

On our last evening, I asked John about school.

'I've just left,' he said.

'So have I. I mean, where are you going?'

'A school in Dorset.'

'Dorset!'

'Bryanston.'

'Bryanston!' I cried. 'So am I! Well, I hope I am. If they can find a space for me.'

'My father and Beryl think it's for the best,' said John, 'because they're divorced. Sally goes to Cranborne Chase.'

The idea that a child might be sent away to school by way of protection or compensation was a new one to me. That wasn't the reason why my parents, who both subscribed to the boarding school system, had sent me to Swanbourne; but the practical effect of doing so was, I suppose, to offer me remission from the home front and a certain stability denied to Sally.

At this moment, my father appeared at the doorstep of the railway carriage, and Beryl swooped on him with delight. 'Peter! Darling!'

My father smiled peaceably, with the air of one for whom no amount of compliments could possibly be too many.

'Kevin,' he said quietly. 'Sally. Dinner.'

Without protesting, we obediently stood up. The Richters looked at us like poor, pitiable wretches.

'I'll see you at Bryanston,' I told John. 'I hope I will.'

Because it was our last evening, Neenie had roasted a chicken and Grandpa Frank produced a bottle of Asti Spumante and six such pretty glasses with hollow stems.

Next morning, I got up even earlier than Neenie, eager for

one last look at the creek.

To my horror, I saw Grandpa Frank still sitting in his armchair beside the fire, fully clothed. I thought he was dead.

The room reeked of cigar smoke. And of burning.

Then my grandfather snorted. He began to snore.

Mightily relieved, I took a step closer and looked down at him. He had dropped his half-smoked cigar and it had burnt a hole in the arm of his chair. I retreated upstairs and woke Neenie.

Sally and I did not present ourselves in Grandpa Frank's bedroom later that morning. Neenie said it would be better not to disturb him and gave us our customary farewell gifts herself: a £1 note for me and a ten-shilling note for Sally.

I kissed my grandmother and climbed into the car, content that I was going to see her again later in the holidays, but apprehensive about how she, Sally and I would all be able to fit into the back of our new Beetle for a journey halfway across Europe.

On a Shoestring

The cover of my log of our holiday in Switzerland in August 1954 is lovingly decorated with familiar emblems: a luge, a pair of skis, a yellow-stamened gentian, an elegant watch, a low-slung chalet backed by a freezing lake and wave upon wave of mountains; and also, less predictably, with what appears to be a peach with a large bite taken out of it.

Inside, bald as a paragraph in the *Anglo-Saxon Chronicle*, the first entry reports that on 4 August we drove up to London, en route for Dover, met Neenie there 'for five minutes' – she had come down from Norfolk by train – 'and then went to Broadcasting House and had a big tea before my broadcast. My partner was Wendy Humfries. At 5.15 p.m. we began Regional Round, and were equal 2nd with 10pts against North's 11pts. After that, all of us met "David"(Davis) . . . We were each given a 10/6 book token.'

What this omits is how, in this *Children's Hour* quiz between pairs of children from the different regions, I told Wendy to leave all the musical questions to me, because music was the one subject I really knew about, only to fail to identify 'On Ilkley Moor baht'at'. What it omits is my father's part in arranging for me to appear on the programme, and my feverish excitement and anxiety.

This was our second visit to the Valais in successive years. The previous summer, we had driven out to Arolla, and our last overnight stop was in Evian.

All afternoon, cooped up in our little car, I'd been increasingly rebellious, and then I went too far, informing my mother and father that I wished I didn't have to go on holiday with them and Sally, and I couldn't put up with them for the next two weeks.

My mother glared at my father, and he pulled up. 'In that case, Kevin,' he said in his measured voice, 'when we get to the hotel, you can go straight to your room and miss supper, and stay there until tomorrow morning.'

Later, Sally interceded with my parents and brought me up a tray of soup, half a baguette and a glass of water, and put it down on my bed. I was so angry that I picked up the baguette and threw it at her. Poor Sally fled down the wide flight of stairs, crying.

Sally and I were each given a special holiday allowance of one franc per day and, perhaps partly as a peace offering, my father unwisely presented me at breakfast next morning with the whole of my first week's allowance. Before we had even reached Arolla, I'd spent the lot (and a bit more, borrowed from Sally) on a Swiss army penknife. By the second day, I regretted how impulsive I had been; and late each afternoon during the following week, I stood outside our hotel, accosting guests as they returned from their day's outings, trying in vain to sell my penknife to them!

While we were staying at Arolla, a glamorous young American woman, Bertha Milich, struck up a friendship with us, and more especially with my father. She hiked with us, painted watercolours with us, ate with us, and what began as the usual kind of pleasant holiday acquaintanceship became, in my mother's eyes, altogether too much of a good thing.

Matters took a turn for the worse when Bertha enthralled

Sally and me by presenting each of us with a large set of Caran d'Ache pencils.

One morning, Sally was sewing a button on to her dress, and asked my mother how to tie the thread to round things off.

'Oh! Go and ask Bertha,' my mother snapped. 'She'll know.' Sally still remembers being taken aback by how abrupt, how tart my mother sounded.

In my little album of 'Snapshots', there's a picture of Mont Collon I took from the grounds of our hotel. I describe it as being 15,000 feet high, and I knew perfectly well that this was an exaggeration when I wrote it. Beneath it, I've written 'THIS IS THE BEST PHOTO I HAVE EVER TAKEN'. In my mother's album, meanwhile, there is another of my photographs. My father basks in the foreground; next to him, Sally perches on an outcrop, squinting into the camera; and between them is Bertha, bare-shouldered, bronzed. My mother is sitting on her own, well behind the others, and she looks absolutely fed up.

In the event, Bertha became a family friend, almost an installation. She came to stay with us in Whiteleaf the following April, sent me presents at Swanbourne (a sketchbook, a set of darts, a book of recorder music) and spent several Christmases with us after we had moved to London.

One reason why my mother invited Neenie to join us on our second trip to Switzerland may have been by way of indemnity – with his own mother in tow, my father was unlikely to discover another Bertha.

Neenie was suffering from increasingly painful arthritis, and my mother proposed mixing business with pleasure by staying at Leukerbad so that Neenie could go to the thermal baths there.

After the previous year's trip to Arolla, our resources were depleted and, instead of staying in a hotel, we rented a chalet. Our rooms were immediately above the family's cowshed, the normal arrangement in many a chalet. According to my log, it rained almost all the time, but this didn't deter Neenie from proceeding to the thermal baths, where she spent an hour each day (the water was 125°F/52°C) and professed to feel better because of it.

True, my log is packed with the customary small, almost unchanging delights and incidents: eating wild strawberries, seeing *Heidi* in the village cinema, the clanking and clunking of cowbells, collecting pails of frothy milk, playing whist, watching the goatherd and a whole crowd of pursuers vainly try to retrieve a bounding mountain goat, slipping and falling into a sizzling, cold, stony mountain stream while I was 'trying to cross it for the sixth time', listening to the town band, buying plates for our walking sticks, picnics, sketching, hiking to the top of the Gemmi Pass and being rewarded by immense views. But for all this, Sally and I both remember our holiday in Leukerbad as being not only sopping but somehow blighted.

A packet of letters arrived but, frustratingly, not the crucial and long-awaited one from Thorold Coade to let us know whether he could find a place for me at Bryanston.

Sally twisted her foot; then she tried to stroke a Saint Bernard and it bit her, and she had to go to the doctor in case she had rabies; I kept throwing up; then I got diarrhoea; my father had a fever, and he and I swapped beds so that he could sleep in a room on his own. There was a great deal of temperature-taking.

It was only when we made a raid into Italy over the Simplon Pass that the clouds lifted. My log is bathed in brilliant sunshine, and reports of eating dinner beneath a trellis draped with swags of grapes, and languidly rowing on Lake Orta and inspecting the skeleton in the church of Saint Julius. But, actually, we only stayed in Italy for a single night, and that speaks for itself. The whole holiday was done on a shoestring.

Everything was carefully planned – by my mother, inevitably – so that Neenie wouldn't be worn out in the back of the Beetle (we only once covered as much as 250 miles in one day) and so we would have an opportunity to sightsee en route. On the way home, we visited Vézelay and Chartres, where my father took me to a late-night concert in the cathedral (beginning, I noted, at 9.15 p.m.) of trios by Beethoven, Mendelssohn and Lalo. We didn't get back to our hotel until after 11p.m. I felt grown-up.

Our arrival in Rouen coincided with the tenth anniversary of the city's liberation, and the whole place was *en fête*, complete with runners arriving hotfoot from Paris at the Monument of Victory, carrying flaming torches. With her usual attention to detail, my mother had arranged for us to stay in a hotel in Rue de l'Horloge right next to the renowned clock tower 'so you can hear it striking in your sleep'; but in the event, the street was packed all night with revellers, volleyball players, musicians, drunks.

Once they turn for home, travellers tend to quicken their pace, and want to get back as soon as they can. Not my mother. Our progress remained measured, and after reaching Dover we found time to visit Canterbury Cathedral.

When we came to the tomb of the Black Prince, I remembered how he had visited his manor at 'Riseburgh' in 1359, and how Princes Risborough is named after him. Then my father reminded Sally and me how he had married our ancestor, Joan Holland, John of Gaunt's niece, and I thought of her statuette, lit up in the dining-room alcove at Rahere. The Black Prince? Why, he almost felt like one of the family.

Picture a newly cut, sweeping lawn. It is just after dawn. Now the sun rises and, to your astonishment and delight, you see that the whole expanse in front of you is covered with gossamer: an immense, intricate, shining web.

Standing beside the tomb of the Black Prince, I began to shiver. And ever since, I've been aware of the network of the quick and the dead. Some strands are knotted with blood; some are the links of love, friendship or acquaintance; some are of philosophical or religious belief; some of profession, enquiry, persuasion, cause; many are links of place; and a few, a very few, are unpredictable and wholly wonderful. Pure chance; unreasonable coincidence.

Children of the technological web, many of us are used to

making worldwide connections; we do so daily and take it for granted. But the silken strands I have in mind are something altogether more mysterious and numinous, less logical, essentially personal. They are our hidden roads.

At Liverpool Street, we saw my beloved Neenie on to the train to Hunstanton. Then my father called in at the BBC; I had my hair cut.

On the mat at Crosskeys lay the letter my parents and I had been waiting for so long. It was from the headmaster of Bryanston, Thorold Coade: blue ink on blue notepaper.

At the eleventh hour, he wrote, there had been one cancellation. He did not know what alternative arrangements my parents might now have made for me but, if they were still interested . . .

My mother looked at me, bright-eyed and jubilant. My father smiled and closed his eyes.

'Your boy,' concluded Mr Coade, 'I'll take a chance on him.'

Thresholds: Before and After

A friend told me about Google Earth. On my computer I typed 'Whiteleaf, Buckinghamshire, England' and asked its engines to search . . .

Within a minute, like a glider gone mad, I was swerving and swooping above the Cross, surveying the Vale of Aylesbury, then staring up at the hill from below.

I guided myself towards Crosskeys. There it was, nestling under the hill. There it waited. My eyeballs grew hot . . . I began to feel queasy. Before long, I was violently sick.

With words so succinct and associative as to achieve the condition of poetry, this is how the Anglo-Saxon *ealdormann* Æthelfrith identified his land in the Monks Risborough Charter of AD 903:

> These are the land-boundaries. First, from the gore into the black hedge. From that hedge on and down into the foul brook. From the foul brook to the west of the ash-tree on the bank, and from there into the old ditch to the west of the herdsman's hut. From that ditch up on to the ridge of the wood on Eadric's boundary. Along Eadric's boundary to the boundary of the Kimble-folk. Along that

boundary to Icknield. Along Icknield as far as the heathen burial-place, and from there along king's street. Up that street to Welland's tree-stump. Down from that stump following the roe-deer fence. Then to the hay glade. From that glade downwards so as to come back to the gore.

Witnessed by royalty and bishops, Monks Risborough is in fact the earliest certified parish boundary in the country and, *mirabile dictu*, several of the markers named above have endured for eleven hundred years and more, and have staked their place in this memoir.

In common with several other local parishes, it was long and thin, its shape determined by the economics of the landscape. For centuries parishioners fed their pigs and collected timber on the hill top, and on the high slopes quarried chalk and flint and gathered brushwood; on the lower slopes, they grew crops while below the spring line they grazed their animals and grew osiers.

And if Æthelfrith were once more to stand on top of Whiteleaf Hill, beside the oval Neolithic burial-mound,* or to peer into my trembling screen, it would not look wholly unfamiliar. True, he would be amazed at how far the forest carpet on the valley floor had been pushed back and would rub his eyes at the number of settlements and even at the oldest cottages in the village of Whiteleaf at his feet, some timber-framed and whitewashed or colourwashed, some incorporating nuggets of flint. (The village may once have been called 'Whitecliff' but it was already known as 'Whytleyff' by 1540.) Æthelfrith would puzzle over the 'jazz-modern' (so say John

* The 1945 excavation revealed in the centre of the mound a small wooden chamber containing an intact left foot, that of a thirty-five-year-old man. Further excavation, between 2002 and 2006, showed that what began as a mortuary structure in the thirty-seventh century BC, the oldest manmade feature in the Chilterns, evolved as 'the result of a sequence of ditch digging and mound construction spanning around 500 years'.

Betjeman and John Piper) design of the Roman Catholic church in Princes Risborough – the component 'Ris' probably derives from the Anglo-Saxon *hris*: brushwood. He would scowl at the smoking cement works at Chinnor but would recognise the Upper Icknield Way running above the spring line, and the Lower crossing the open Vale, and Bledlow Ridge with its Iron Age settlement and, to the west, the abounding, astounding Black Hedge, containing no fewer than twenty-one species, and probably dating from the eighth century.

What of the chalk cross at Æthelfrith's feet? Given that the first representation of it dates from 1742 (where it is entitled 'Crux Saxonica'), is it relatively modern? If it existed for centuries before this, why is there no reference to it in earlier sources? After all, no fewer than seven counties are visible from it and, almost incredibly, you can see it from the White Horse at Uffington, near Swindon. And again, was the Cross a Christian conversion of a way marker or an earlier carving with religious significance? Was it a 'FALLIC SYMBOL', as I captioned the drawing in my museum? Was there already a hill-carving here in Æthelfrith's time? Is he the man who converted it into a cross?

> When I'm standing on top . . . I sometimes think of all the people, all the generations who grew up on this ground, and grew into this ground, their days and years. My Welsh grandmother Nain says the sounds trees make are the voices of the dead and when I listen to the beech trees, they sound like whispering spirits – they're my great-uncles and great-great-aunts, my great-great-great-grand-parents, green again and guiding me. [*]

Many of the people in these pages have gone to ground; a few are still alive.

Grandpa Frank regretted he had not attended university as a young man and, in addition to his many other achievements,

---

[*] From *Arthur: The Seeing Stone*.

he took two science degrees (Licence and Doctorate) in his later years from the University of Nancy, as well as becoming Vice-Chancellor of the Intercollegiate University. He was an active freemason, and less than a year before he died he received holy orders in the Old English Catholic Church (one of the Churches unified in the Western Orthodox Christian Church).

Among his father's papers, my father found these sixteen lines, probably written by my grandfather some years before he died:

> *Dona Nobis Domine*
> (A Hymn of Prayer)
>
> Lord grant us Life, eternal, blessed, free,
> Grant us a holy Life, Lord, lived for Thee.
>
> Lord grant us Light – divine, redeeming ray –
> To guide us more and more to perfect day.
>
> Lord grant us Grace, that we may thankful be,
> For good and perfect gifts that flow from Thee.
>
> Lord grant us Faith; and strengthen our belief:
> Place Thou Thine everlasting arms beneath.
>
> Lord grant us Hope; and wipe away all tears,
> Hope to sustain us in life's closing years.
>
> Lord grant us Love – Thine own rich gift divine,
> That lifts our human nature unto Thine.
>
> Lord grant us Peace – when earthly life shall close
> – Peace passing understanding – Thy repose!
>
> Lord grant us Joy – forgiveness of all sin –
> The joy of Thy 'Well done, enter thou in!'

In 1956, while driving at his customary 29 mph, my Grandpa Frank was badly upset at being overtaken by a dozen buzzing motorcyclists. He had a stroke and suffered a second stroke the following spring. During the summer holidays, my father and I went up to Overy Staithe to see him and Neenie. At one point my grandfather asked Neenie: 'Who is that handsome boy who comes to see me?' 'Frank,' she replied, 'it's your grandson.' My grandfather died peacefully of heart failure and cerebral thrombosis on 27 August.

When my father spoke to his mother on the phone, she reported of Grandpa Frank, lying on his bed, 'He looks noble.' And later, my father (then in Edinburgh) noted how on the night of 27 August, he had a profound sense of communicating with his father, as though he were asking, 'What can I do for you?' My father continues: 'At that time I was deeply involved in metaphysical studies and my dearest wish was to find, and be able to write, a music passing all ordinary experience; and on the instant the answer arose deep within me: "I want to hear the music of God." And the response immediately followed, taking some time: this music was now *laid down* in me – it seemed like a subtle yet deep physical implantation – but even as this "happened", I knew that I would hear that music only at the time of my own death.'

Neenie told Sally and me that she hoped she would survive Grandpa Frank and have 'a few quiet years'. In the event, she lived for a further twenty-three. She delighted in her children and grandchildren, especially the males of the species. For as long as I was at school, she continued to send me almost weekly letters and supplies to top up my tuck box. Towards the end of her life, she retreated for the winter months to a hotel in Brighton so as to be near her son Dick and his wife Rosemary, but she lived at Rahere for the remainder of the year, seeing a small circle of friends, pruning her roses, pickling shallots and samphire, knitting brightly coloured patchwork rugs, feeding the birds, rejoicing in flights of wild geese, donning her sea-lavender tweed suit and trooping over the hill to Burnham Overy church, and welcoming her family. When she was ninety, Neenie and I walked all seven legs of Burnham Dyke, and then slogged over the two waves of dunes. The tide was running, and the north wind sprang up to meet us.

Back in the cottage, we lit the fire.

'I'm ready to die now,' my grandmother said.

I was still young enough for this to sound dismaying. I told Neenie I hoped she'd live for ever and that I'd never be able to come to Overy Staithe without thinking of her.

'I've lived long enough,' my grandmother concluded.

> Under the cowl, out on Scolt Head
> The swell and swash are inching their way back.
> The water picks up pebbles, razor shells,
> Birds' small bleached bones and witches' purses;
> It toys with them, cries over them,
> And the legendary wave embraces them.
> The tide returning: each wave and whisker,
> Everything forged into one force,
> A fusion with one meaning and purpose.
> But I think you are going further,
> Ancient shuffler, at the fire now, flushed
> By this last blaze before going to bed.[*]

Neenie died on 26 February 1979. She was ninety-four.

My uncle Dick taught French for many years at Brighton College, punctuated by a period of eight years (1971–9) when he served as headmaster of Hawkhurst Court, the College's preparatory school at Wisborough Green. He died in 1995, and his ashes are interred in the churchyard at Burnham Thorpe.

Dick is survived by my aunt Rosemary, in whose company I have always delighted, and by their three children, Andrew, Jonathan and Carolyn.

Education, service, dry wit, a sense of family and a passion for north Norfolk run in their blood. Andrew has recently retired as headteacher of a large primary school in Kent, Jonathan has been the Education Officer for the city of Sheffield, and is now Director of Children's Services for the Tribal Group, and Carolyn is a counsellor in the National

---

[*] *Selected Poems*: from 'Neenie'.

Health Service and private practice, and an executive coach.

In a fine 1977 San Francisco lecture, my father spoke of how he had always believed that music 'could open the door to a fuller life, a life where things happened in proper order':

> At first I felt this in the great classical music on which I was nurtured . . . Many influences came to play their part. For instance, I steeped myself in the traditional music of the Celtic peoples, with whose mystery and beauty I felt a deep affinity. I received a new stimulus from listening to and playing medieval music, and I tried to penetrate the secrets of the Gothic cathedral composers, the troubadours and the Christian saints. Each of these traditions had evidently tried to build a bridge to that other life I sought. [*]

This search is reflected in what have generally been taken to be my father's finest compositions: following *The Sacred Dance*, effectively an extended carol for baritone, chorus and orchestra in which Jesus recounts his life, punctuated by the refrain 'This have I done for my true love', he wrote *Des Puys d'Amors* (1955–6), a dramatic song cycle for baritone, violin and string orchestra based on troubadour and trouvère themes, and for the same forces *Reis Glorios* (a dawn song on a twelfth-century theme). My father then composed a tender and beautiful five-movement cantata, *The Visions of Saint Godric*, to words by the early medieval saint who lived much of his life as a hermit in the woods at Finchale near Durham. Janet Baker was one of the soloists at the first performance in 1959.

So what of my parents' decision to remain married, and to live under one roof, until Sally and I were grown up? They honoured it, they endured it until we were nineteen and twenty-two respectively.

One October morning in 1963, after breakfast, my mother went to the front door of our house in West Hampstead to see

* Reprinted in *Speaking of My Life*, edited by Jacob Needleman

my father off to a UNESCO conference in Berlin.

'Goodbye, Joan,' he said in his measured, gentle voice. 'I . . . I won't be coming back.'

So unprepared, as ever, to face the music; so brutal.

My mother staggered into the kitchen, and her legs gave way beneath her.

Earlier in the year, my father had left his job as Third Programme Music Organiser at the BBC where, as his obituary in *The Times* noted, he had been 'responsible for introducing into the schedules Indian and other non-Western musics'. There was one memorable evening in West Hampstead when our guests included Ravi Shankar and the Indian dancer Indrani, who had been Miss India two years before. I sat at her feet, and wished the evening would last for ever.

After leaving my mother, my father moved to Berlin where he was assistant director of the Institute for Music Research for a couple of years, and won recognition for his two discs of Tibetan sacred music (made in Bhutan and Ladakh seven years before) issued by Bärenreiter as part of UNESCO's 'A Musical Anthology of the Orient' series.

This is how his obituary in *The Times* continues and concludes:

> Then, after teaching assignments at American universities, he was in 1969 appointed Professor of Music (ethnomusicology) at the University of California at Los Angeles (taking what had been Schoenberg's chair). Generations of students in California were delighted by the wonders of traditional music and instruments from all over the world.
>
> During his years in Berlin and America, composition inevitably took a back seat, but his contribution to ethnomusicology was immense, particularly his writings on and field studies of the musical traditions of Tibet, and his investigations into the musical artefacts of pre-Columbian America.

On his retirement from UCLA in 1983 Crossley-Holland returned to Britain and settled in his beloved Wales, where he continued his research into Celtic music and folklore, as well as resuming composition.

His later works include a symphony (as yet unperformed), three symphonic poems, and an *Ode to Mananan* for recorder, string orchestra and harp, inspired by Manx folklore, which was given its premiere in March by the Welsh Chamber Orchestra. At the time of his sudden death (after attending an 80th birthday party for Denys Darlow who for many years had been a great protagonist of his music) he was engaged in scoring for string orchestra his song *The Philosopher Bird*, which was composed to words by his son.

In 1992, in recognition of his contribution to Welsh music studies, he was made an Honorary Fellow of the University of Wales, Bangor, which published his recent research into the composers of the Robert ap Huw manuscript. The university was also the recipient of part of his large collection of musical instruments.

Peter Crossley-Holland's first marriage, to Joan Cowper in 1939, was dissolved. He is survived by his second wife, Nicole, and by the son and daughter of his first marriage.

My father had met Nicole, née Marzac, in England. A medievalist and palaeographer, she was teaching at London University. Later, she held a professorship in the University of California. Her books include a fascinating study of the household of a fourteenth-century knight, *Living and Dining in Medieval Paris*.

In 1948, my father edited a collection of essays, *Music in Wales*. He began his introduction with words that spoke to the heart, and that once I knew by heart:

The birds of Rhiannon sang to the seven warriors of the Island of the Mighty a certain song, and all the songs that they had ever heard were unpleasant compared thereto, and the singing was so sweet that the warriors remained spellbound for eighty years together listening to the birds.

My father was eighty-five when he died on 27 April 2001, and throughout his life he had listened to the birds of Rhiannon, and was deeply interested in descriptions and the occasional notation of music in traditional tales, especially Welsh fairy-tales. He lived in a kind of *zwischenplatz* between actuality and dream.

Sons and daughters are by no means necessarily the best assessors of extra-marital and subsequent marital relationships made by their parents. But what Sally and I readily recognise is that my father's relationship with Nicole was loving and play-ful and enriched by a deep reciprocal interest in one another's work. It lasted for over forty years, and that, I realise, is almost twice as long as my mother and father lived together.

Abandoned by my father, my mother decided to lick her wounds well away from her immediate family. She rapidly secured a position as Personal Assistant to the Maharana of Mewar and as manager of his fabled Lake Palace Hotel in Udaipur in Rajasthan.

For a year, she threw herself into this challenge with her cus-tomary zest, though it's plain she was sometimes lonely and homesick. Enclosing little blue-green feathers, she wrote bril-liant weekly letters to Sally and me, perfect instances of early magical realism:

> Let me give you some impression of this unbelievable, oriental, feudal, wild country, where princes are wor-shipped and officiate as God-priests in their temples; where 'might is right' and 'the ends sanctify the means'; where Figaro and the Barber of Seville flourish in their master's pay, curling the nobles' moustaches, arranging their dancing girls, their concerts and their intrigues, while the marble and plaster palaces crumble about their

ears in these sunset years. The opposite banks of the lake are roamed by spotted deer, blue boar, monkey, brown bear, panther and tiger. The lake is full of flat pink fish that jump into the air – as well they might considering they share its waters with turtle, crab and water snake, iguana and crocodile. And on the trees peacocks balance in the wind, whilst a thousand, thousand green parakeets wing their way home from the surrounding hills and roost in noisy crowds each evening on the nearby island palace ruin; whilst around the water's edge storks meditate, ibis fish, green pigeons fluster, and blue swallows with brown heads and white bodies and sad curlews skim the water. Each night the flying foxes flounder across the lake in an ungainly, ominous black cloud from the trees of the deserted gardens of the palace; and the vultures, like rag bags on the tall palms, wait for us all to die.

When my mother came back to England, she did so with a clear sense of purpose: to encourage and promote the work of contemporary craft. First she was appointed director of the Bear Lane Gallery in Oxford; and then, after a row with the trustees, she upped sticks in 1968 and, henching herself with strong and able women, founded the celebrated Oxford Gallery.

Later, she wrote: 'Perhaps before memories sweeten with time's passing, I should clearly state for the sake of hopeful initiates that gallery-owning is not a charming, sophisticated and elegant way of gaining a living to the sound of trumpets. It involves more capital than you calculated you would ever need to forward the work of artists you admire but who don't necessarily reciprocate your feelings, and persuading some mildly interested visitor to curtail his annual holiday by two weeks or so in order to afford "a dish fit for a king" by a craftsman he had not even heard of one hour ago. Finding out how to do this will absorb the rest of your life!'

It did absorb most of the rest of my mother's life. Between

1968 and 1986, she mounted 187 exhibitions and displayed the work of over 2000 craftsmen and fine artists, who remember her with just about every emotion, ranging from very great affection and passionate admiration to terror. Like her own mother Mary, decorated for organising nursing supplies for the Front during the First World War, she was awarded an MBE (for services to the arts).

My mother did not make another love-relationship. She was a one-man woman and remained deeply fond of, and in a sense committed to, my father throughout her life. After retiring at the age of seventy-four, she lived in the Domesday Book village of Walsham-le-Willows in Suffolk, where I was living at the time:

> She would still enjoy a head-to-head
> with Heidegger, but not the waiting for it.
> Her ardour for the sensual kept well in check
> (say, chaste Lucie Rie) is no less pronounced
> than it ever was, and her rejection
> of the less than excellent uncompromising.
> A gift for metaphor – and a sense
> of humour. I can praise this woman!
> But anxieties make her hoarse: her health;
> the whole estate of her children. Her hair
> is silver and ash, and downy as a cygnet.
> Today she told me that on her constitutional
> – and all day golden rods and storm clouds,
> charcoal and indigo, and swirling leaves –
> she counted her soft steps. One by one.
> 'Two thousand three hundred and ten,' she said.
> True, she went on to ruminate on aspects
> of the mile, beginning with the stride
> of the centurion. But how easily she tires.
> She sips and sups no more than a sparrow.
> Is this how she begins to simplify:
> counting and recounting the sum of her steps?*

* *Selected Poems*: 'Counting Her Steps'.

For the last three years of her life, my mother lived in a nursing home near Bury St Edmunds, and her death in January 2005 occasioned substantial obituaries in *The Times*, *The Guardian* and *The Independent*. The legend on her York headstone in the churchyard of Walsham-le-Willows reads: 'Valiant in her perseverance, generous in her vision'.

My sister Sally dearly loved her riding lessons with strong, dutiful Miss Llewelyn and tells me that it was a toss-up whether to pursue horsemanship or dance, given that our parents could not afford to send her to public school. 'Mummy's and Daddy's first thought was what on earth to do with me,' she says. 'Something where you couldn't compete with me.' In the event, Sally attended the Ballet Rambert school in Notting Hill Gate throughout her early teens, and only relinquished her ambition to be a dancer when, despite cortisone injections, the joints of her feet became too painful. Benedict Rubbra painted an arresting portrait of her as a ballet student.

Curiously, her marriage to Richard (Dick) Poulton soon took her to Bryanston, and their three children were educated there. Thereafter, Dick served for six years as Headmaster at Wycliffe College and for all but ten at Christ's Hospital, the school I so nearly went to. In each instance, Sally was his busy, immensely able, working (i.e. salaried) partner.

When I see her, surrounded by husband and children and grandchildren, I see a fulfilment in family, for all its frustrations, denied to her mother and her mother's mother.

Loving and loyal, instinctive and outspoken, generous to a fault, she is the best of sisters. She has often added to and corrected my memory-hoard while I've been writing this memoir, and it is dedicated to her.

There it is. I hope my hidden roads will be well frequented. Above all, I hope my four children, Kieran and Dominic, Oenone and Eleanor, will want to read these pages about their father's childhood, and will discover the ways, sometimes gratifying, sometimes galling, but anyhow tantalising, in which family characteristics disappear and reappear and reassert themselves.

To-day I know there is nothing beyond the farthest of far ridges except a signpost to unknown places. The end is in the means – in the sight of that beautiful long straight line of the Downs in which a curve is latent – in the houses we shall never enter, with their dark secret windows and quiet hearth smoke, or their ruins friendly only to elders and nettles – in the people passing whom we shall never know though we may love them . . . I could not find a beginning or an end of the Icknield Way. It is thus a symbol of mortal things with their beginnings and ends always in immortal darkness.'

Edward Thomas: The Icknield Way (dedication)

Acknowledgements

With research and information, opinion and hospitality, a good number of my family and friends as well as several institutions have refined and leavened this short memoir. I'm especially grateful to Ronald Blythe, the Buckinghamshire County Museum, Gillian Crossley-Holland, Rosemary Crossley-Holland, Lynda and Henry Edwardes-Evans, Judith Elliott, Sally Festing, Geoffrey Findlay, Sandy and Elizabeth Macfarlane and the Princes Risborough Area Heritage Society, Carla and the late Bernard Phillips, John Richter, Peter Smith, Carolyn Turnbull, Ann Walker and Wycombe Museum.

I owe Anthony Cheetham great gratitude for his unflagging and zestful support for my writing, and it has been a delight to work for the first time with my editor, Roisin Heycock and her colleagues, Parul Bavishi and Nicci Praca, and Lucie Ewin of Rook Books. I'm also indebted to my poetry publisher, Stephen Stuart-Smith, for allowing me to draw so liberally on my *Selected Poems* (Enitharmon Press), and to Orion Children's Books for permission to reprint passages from *The Seeing Stone* (the first volume in my Arthur trilogy). All the poetry and prose quotations in the text are from my own writing unless otherwise specified.

John Nash's watercolour, "Whiteleaf Woods", is reproduced by kind permission of Claudia Wolfers and the artistic estate of John Nash; the photograph of 'Whiteleaf Hill and Cross', by Andy Rafferty; the view from the top of Whiteleaf Cross, by Alison Doggett; the snapshot of the Findlay family, by Ann Walker and Geoffrey Findlay; the photograph of Gun Hill, by permission of Nicolette Hallett and Orlando Publishing, Norwich; Emile Cardinaux's poster design for 'L'Été en Suisse', by permission of L'Office National Suisse du Tourisme; and the Bodgers' work-site, by permission of Wycombe Museum. I am most grateful to David Leighton and the estate of Clare Leighton for permission to reproduce images from *Four Hedges* by way of my section headings as well as Clare Leighton's wood engravings of *A Lapful of Windfalls* and *Whiteleaf Cross*. I have made every attempt to contact the copyright holders of text and images reproduced in this book, and will be pleased to hear from any who have escaped me.

Not for the first time, Twiggy Bigwood has picked her way through the wildwood of my manuscript and typed many successive drafts with great skill and good humour. My wife Linda has once again helped me to organise a text as well as making many perceptive and sensitive comments on it – no one could reasonably expect such loving patience and support. And lastly, my generous sister Sally's 'insider opinion', and her memory of events I'd forgotten and others I never knew, has been utterly invaluable. My story has been part of hers, and hers part of mine.